To Marie
Culinary Greetings
Exec Sous. Chef [signature]

Thank you for
Cruising with us.

Royal Caribbean International
Executive Chef
Liberty of the Seas

SAVOR

The Royal Caribbean International Cookbook

Volume 2

Dear Guest,

Welcome to our 2nd edition of *Savor*, Royal Caribbean International's tribute to the culinary arts and talent throughout our fleet. Due to popular demand, we have extended our recipes from our 1st edition, Cordon d' Or gold ribbon-awarded *Savor*, into this new and improved version. We have also taken the suggestions of our readers to add new features to our book such as new wine pairings, degree of difficulty ratings and the addition of metric conversions.

Savor invites you to sail with us as we take you on a culinary journey like no other. Our team of esteemed chefs from around the globe will help you navigate your kitchen to create meals that make your taste buds dance, and inspire your culinary creativity!

Savor features our guest's favorite recipes from the Royal Caribbean International fleet and our innovative menus on board. This book reflects the dedication, creativity and professionalism of our Executive Chefs and Food & Beverage Teams. The fabulous dishes and fan-fare you have enjoyed while sailing with us are now at your fingertips!

You will meet our chefs and their own personal favorite recipes. This book also features interesting culinary facts and history, wine pairings and enticing cocktails.

We invite you to sample the dishes and recipes during your cruise, not only in our main dining rooms, but also in our internationally acclaimed specialty restaurants, Chops and Portofino and to relax and unwind while tasting our cocktails and espresso beverages at our various bars and coffee shops.

In addition to all that, if you're lucky, the Executive Chefs featured in this book may be on board your cruise. Seek them out and have your book signed. It's a great opportunity to chat and get some unique and fascinating insight on what happens behind the scenes when producing 15,000 meals per day with fresh, natural ingredients. Did you know that we bake all our breads, produce all our cakes and desserts, and create new pieces of art out of fruit, ice and chocolate daily, right on board? Were you aware of the fact that our chefs and cooks hail from over 50 countries, making ours the most diverse infusion of international culinary talent on or off the seven seas? And did you know that Royal Caribbean International has been partnered for the past 3 years with the American Culinary Federation, to train and certify all of our chefs and cooks at the highest standards? Since the introduction of the program, more than 100 Executive Chefs, Executive Sous Chefs and Sous Chefs have been certified. In 2008, 400 more cooks and chefs are planning to achieve their certification—a clear testament of the commitment to culinary excellence by our employees.

Whether recreating one of our magnificent Chef's Signature dishes or indulging in one of our delectable desserts, this book will get you cooking like a world class chef! We have a world of talent to share, so let the adventure begin in your kitchen and continue on your next Royal Caribbean International Cruise!

Bon Voyage and Bon Appétit!

Frank Weber
Vice President, Food & Beverage Operations
Royal Caribbean International

SAVOR

The Royal Caribbean International Cookbook

Volume 2

Welcome to *Savor Volume 2*, the cookbook that introduces you to the executive chefs of Royal Caribbean International and their signature dishes.

From tantalizing starters to scrumptious main courses to delectable desserts, 30 chefs from across the Royal Caribbean fleet present a diverse selection of recipes from around the world that are perfect for all tastes. And, our chefs offer their recommendations for the perfect wine to accompany each dish to further enhance the dining experience.

Go "all Asian" with Executive Chef Markus Zihlmann's *Shrimp Udon* and move on to a main course of succulent *Asian Duck* from Senior Executive Chef Thomas Pfennings. Finish the meal with *Asian Poached Pears with Chocolate Truffles and Caramel Lichees*, a luscious creation of Corporate Pastry Chef Romeo Bueno.

Or, create a savory Italian feast with a traditional *Caesar Salad*, *Grilled Vegetable Antipasti* and *Tagliatelli con Coppa* from Executive Chef Martin Grabenhoffer. End the meal with our signature dessert sampler *Dolcetti Alla Portofino*.

Of course, you can always mix up your menu, sampling from over 110 of our very best recipes in this beautifully photographed book.

While the fare within these pages is decidedly gourmet, all recipes are straightforward and simple to prepare. Working with ingredients that are easily accessible, *Savor Volume 2* is a cookbook you can turn to again and again for culinary inspiration.

I'd like to add that $1 of your cookbook purchase will benefit the Make-a-Wish Foundation and its noble mission to 'share the power of a wish' with children who have life-threatening medical conditions.

Enjoy!

Adam M. Goldstein

Adam Goldstein
President
Royal Caribbean International

WINES THAT HIT JUST THE RIGHT NOTE

One of the pleasures of cooking fine cuisine is choosing a wine to enhance your meal. As in musical composition, sometimes you may want sweet harmony between the main elements; other times you may want a bold contrast for drama. You are the maestro. So how do you choose?

Wine is as important to fine dining as the meal itself…wine does actually make food taste better. The acidity present in wines awakens the taste buds, unlocking flavors so that the full range can be enjoyed. This doesn't mean more acidity is better; it's all about the balance between the food and the wine. Classic pairings such as shellfish with a buttery Chardonnay, or beef and big red wines always work, but don't be afraid to experiment and find your own favorites.

Consider the texture, feel, aromas and flavors of the food and wine… pair robust wines with rich, hearty foods and light, refreshing wines with delicate foods. Or go for drama…a high-acidity wine like Sauvignon Blanc can unleash even more creamy flavor from a dish like pasta Alfredo. Don't worry about one "right" choice, there are as many choices as there are chefs…and hungry guests.

Naturally, our chefs have their own opinions! We've included some of their suggestions on wine pairings to get you started on composing with confidence. Look for the wine glass throughout the book for the chef's own recommendation. Enjoy!

Vintages Lounge | *Freedom of the*

"A good meal is wholeness, when everything gels. I like it when everything complements each other, including the wines. That's the way we look at performance—it's the contribution to the whole."

— Ramsey Lewis, American jazz musician

TABLE OF Contents

These icons give a rating system for the degree of difficulty in making the recipes in this cookbook.
1= Easiest   5=Most Difficult

♛♛♛♛♛ = 1   ♛♛♛♛♛ = 2   ♛♛♛♛♛ = 3   ♛♛♛♛♛ = 4   ♛♛♛♛♛ = 5

The prelude to our meal came in the form of an artistic expression, introducing us to a theme.

SALADS

1 pound (450 g) fresh Alaskan salmon fillet, skin off, trimmed

MARINADE

1 tablespoon (15 g) anise seeds
1 tablespoon (15 g) coriander seeds
1 tablespoon (15 g) juniper berries
1 tablespoon (15 g) white peppercorn
2 tablespoons (30 g) lemon zest
3 tablespoons (45 g) orange zest
2 tablespoons (30 g) peeled and grated ginger
$^1/_2$ cup (115 g) sugar
$^1/_4$ cup (60 g) salt

DRESSING

1 white onion, finely chopped
1 teaspoon (5 ml) vegetable oil
$^3/_4$ cup (175 ml) soy sauce
2 tablespoons (30 ml) corn oil
2 tablespoons (30 ml) sesame oil
2 tablespoons (30 ml) rice vinegar
Juice of $^1/_2$ orange
1 teaspoon (5 g) sugar
1 teaspoon (5 g) mustard
Salt and freshly ground black pepper

SALAD MIX

3 cups (700 g) organic mesclun mix

GARNISH

4 pansies
$^1/_4$ bunch chervil
$^1/_4$ bunch opal basil
$^1/_4$ bunch chives

CITRUS FRAGRANCED ALASKAN SALMON WITH ORGANIC FIELD GREENS

For marinade, crush anise seeds, coriander, juniper berries and pepper in a mortar, add citrus zests, ginger, sugar and salt, and mix well.

Arrange a large piece of plastic wrap onto a working surface and sprinkle it with half of spice mixture. Lay salmon fillet on top and sprinkle with remaining spice mixture. Wrap tightly into the plastic wrap and refrigerate for 20 hours.

For dressing, over medium heat in a small sauté pan, heat vegetable oil and sauté onion for 3 minutes, until translucent. Transfer to a blender, add remaining ingredients and blend until very fine. Cover and refrigerate.

Toss mesclun with $^1/_2$ of the dressing and slice salmon into 2 inch (5 cm) strips.

To serve, place mesclun on chilled plates and arrange salmon around, drizzle with remaining dressing and garnish with pansies and fresh herbs.

Cooking should be a carefully balanced reflection of all the good things in life. To cultivate a passion for the very best you must commit to prepare and serve only the very best. Every cruise gives us the freedom to tantalize your taste buds.

Josef Jungwirth

Josef Jungwirth,
Director, Culinary Operations, CEC, CCA

Chef Josef joined Royal Caribbean International in March 1999 as Corporate Executive Chef. Josef was born in Koeingwiesen, Austria. At 15, he began a 4-year apprenticeship at Hotel zur Post in St. Valentin, Austria, followed by working as Chef Saucier on Cunard's QE2. He has held numerous positions with Cunard, as well as working in some of the finest restaurants and hotel kitchens in Europe and the United States. Josef also enjoyed a stint with Hyatt International at the Grand Hyatt in Seoul, Korea. Josef is a Master Chef and member of many professional organizations, including the Chaîne des Rôtisseurs, and was awarded the "Culinary Order of Merit" from the World Master Chef's Society.

CROUTONS

4 tablespoons (60 ml) extra virgin olive oil
1 cup (250 g) sourdough bread, cubed
Salt and freshly ground black pepper

INGREDIENTS

3 heads romaine lettuce, washed, dried
and cut lengthwise
1/4 cup (60 g) shaved Parmesan cheese

DRESSING

3 cloves garlic
3 tablespoons (45 ml) freshly squeezed lemon juice
5 anchovy fillets, drained or
2 teaspoons (10 g) anchovy paste
2 teaspoons (10 g) Dijon mustard
2 teaspoons (10 ml) Worcestershire sauce
2 egg yolks
1 cup (240 ml) extra virgin olive oil
Salt

TRADITIONAL CAESAR SALAD

Preheat oven to 380°F or 195°C.

To prepare croutons, place bread on a baking sheet and drizzle with olive oil. Toss well to coat evenly. Season to taste with salt and black pepper. Bake for 10 minutes or until crisp and golden brown. Set aside to cool on a paper towel.

To prepare Caesar dressing, combine all ingredients except oil in a blender or food processor. Blend until smooth. While processing, slowly add oil. Adjust seasoning, cover, and refrigerate.

Place romaine hearts on chilled plates, drizzle with Caesar dressing, and garnish with Parmesan shavings and croutons. Serve immediately.

Serves 6.

CULINARY NOTES:

Contrary to popular belief, Caesar Salad is not named after Julius Caesar, the famed leader of the Roman Empire, but for Chef Caesar Cardoni, famed Italian restaurateur, who created the dish in Tijuana, Mexico in 1924. The original dish called for coddled whole eggs.

BASIL OIL

1 cup (250 g) firmly packed fresh basil leaves
1/2 cup (120 ml) extra virgin olive oil
Salt and freshly ground black pepper to taste

INGREDIENTS

1 pound (450 g) red grape tomatoes,
cut in half if large
1 1/3 cups (350 g) fresh mozzarella bocconcini
2 tablespoons (30 g) julienned basil
2 tablespoons (30 ml) extra virgin olive oil
Salt and freshly ground black pepper

GARNISH

1 1/2 cups (350 g) mesclun mix
Basil leaves
12 edible flowers (optional)

INSALATA CAPRESE
Grape Tomatoes and Baby Mozzarella Salad

Prepare basil oil by blanching basil in a pan of boiling water for 10 seconds. Drain and rinse with cold water. Pat dry with paper towels and transfer to a blender. Add the oil and purée until smooth. Transfer to a small bowl. Season with salt and black pepper. Cover and refrigerate.

Let stand at room temperature for 30 minutes before using.

In a stainless steel bowl mix grape tomatoes, mozzarella, basil and olive oil. Season with salt and pepper.

Place equal amount of tomatoes and mozzarella in each serving dish.

Garnish with mesclun mix drizzled with basil oil.

Finish with basil leaves and flowers.

Serves 6.

CULINARY NOTES:

Mesclun is also called Spring Mix or Field Greens and is a classic French salad mixture. It is usually made up of young greens and shoots, both wild and cultivated. Radicchio, endive, mâche, frisée, dandelion greens and lollo rosso are often used.

CARPACCIO

1/2 pound (250 g) dolphin, skinned and boneless
1/2 pound (250 g) salmon, skinned and boneless
1/2 pound (250 g) sea scallops
1/2 pound (250 g) tuna, skinned and boneless

MARINADE

1 star anise
1/4 teaspoon (1.2 g) cinnamon
1/4 teaspoon (1.2 g) nutmeg
1/4 teaspoon (1.2 g) allspice
1 teaspoon (5 g) tamarind sauce
1 teaspoon (5 ml) white or dark Jamaican rum
2 tablespoons (30 ml) extra virgin olive oil
Juice of 3 limes
Salt and freshly ground black pepper

SALAD

2 ripe mangoes, peeled and julienned
1/2 ripe papaya, peeled and julienned
1/2 teaspoon (2.5 g) chopped jalapeño
1/2 small red onion, finely chopped
3 tablespoons (45 g) chopped cilantro
1 teaspoon (5 g) peeled and grated ginger
2 teaspoons (10 g) brown sugar
Juice of 1 lime
Juice of 1 orange

GARNISH

1/4 bunch cilantro, finely chopped
Freshly ground black pepper

MONTEGO BAY CARPACCIO WITH PAPAYA MANGO SALAD

Samuel Boyd, Executive Chef, CEC

"Chef Sammy", as his colleagues refer to him, comes to us from Montego Bay, Jamaica. Growing up, he was fortunate enough to have excellent schooling enabling him to follow his career choice. He studied at the School of Culinary Arts of Jamaica and graduated at the top of his class. He began his career as an apprentice at the Sandals Royal Caribbean Hotel in Jamaica. In 1989 Samuel joined Commodore Cruise Line's Enchanted Isle where he was promoted to Executive Chef. In 1996 he arrived at Royal Caribbean International where he worked as a Sous Chef and Chef de Cuisine before resuming the position of Executive Chef. During his spare time Samuel enjoys diving and fishing.

Cut fish and scallops in thin slices and arrange on a large plate.

For marinade, mash anise with a mortar and pestle. Combine anise and remaining ingredients in a bowl and mix well. Adjust seasoning with salt and pepper.

Lightly brush marinade over each piece of fish, cover and refrigerate for 2 hours.

For salad, mix mangoes and papaya in a bowl with all ingredients. Cover and refrigerate for 1 hour.

On chilled plates, place a small mound of salad in the center, top with carpaccio and garnish with cilantro. Grind black pepper over plates.

Serves 6.

2 lamb tenderloins, well-trimmed
2 tablespoons (30 ml) extra virgin olive oil

CHARMOULA MARINADE

1/4 cup (60 ml) extra virgin olive oil
1 small red onion, finely chopped
2 cloves garlic, crushed
1/4 teaspoon (1.2 g) peeled and minced ginger
1/4 teaspoon (1.2 g) cumin
1/4 teaspoon (1.2 g) paprika
1/4 teaspoon (1.2 g) chopped coriander
Pinch cayenne pepper
1 teaspoon (5 g) lemon zest
1 teaspoon (5 g) lime zest
1 teaspoon (5 g) orange zest
1 tablespoon (15 g) chopped parsley
1 tablespoon (15 g) chopped rosemary
Juice of 1/2 lemon
Juice of 1/2 lime
Juice of 1/2 orange
2 tablespoons (30 g) honey
Salt and pepper

PEPERONATA

3 tablespoons (45 ml) extra virgin olive oil
3 cloves garlic, crushed
1 red onion cut into strips
1 red bell pepper cut into strips
1 yellow bell pepper, cut into strips
3 Roma tomatoes, peeled, seeded and
cut into strips
1 tablespoon (15 g) chopped rosemary
1 tablespoon (15 g) chopped thyme
Salt and freshly ground black pepper

VINAIGRETTE

1/4 cup (60 ml) rice wine vinegar
2 tablespoons (30 g) chopped mint
1/4 teaspoon (1.2 g) peeled and minced ginger
1/2 tablespoon (7.5 g) honey
1/2 cup (120 ml) vegetable oil
Salt and freshly ground black pepper

1 pound (450 g) mesclun mix

OCEANIC LAMB
TENDERLOIN SALAD

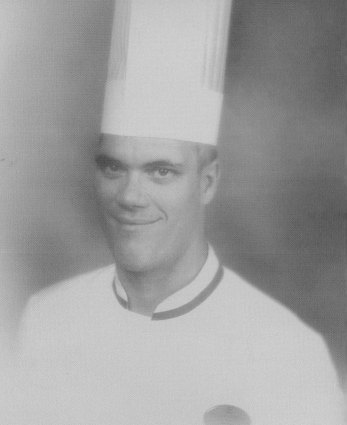

Peter Howell, Executive Chef, CEC

For marinade, heat oil and sauté onion, garlic and ginger for 2 minutes, or until fragrant, in a small saucepan over low heat. Do not brown. Add spices, citrus zests and herbs, and stir well. Remove from heat and let cool. Transfer mixture to a blender. Add citrus juices and honey. Blend for 2 minutes, until very smooth. Adjust seasoning with salt and pepper. Coat tenderloins with marinade, cover and refrigerate for 3 hours.

For peperonata, over medium heat in a sauté pan, heat oil and sauté garlic until fragrant. Do not brown. Add vegetables and sauté for 5 minutes. Stir in herbs and adjust seasoning. Transfer into a non-reactive bowl, cover and refrigerate.

Preheat oven to 300°F or 150°C.

Heat a skillet over high heat. Add oil and reduce heat to medium. Remove lamb from the marinade, shake off excess liquid and sear medallions on all sides for 5 minutes, until nicely browned. Place on a baking sheet and roast in oven for 5 to 7 minutes or until medium pink. Remove from oven and let rest for 10 minutes. Cover and refrigerate for 2 hours.

For vinaigrette, place vinegar, mint, ginger and honey in a blender. Blend over medium-high speed for 2 minutes, until smooth. Reduce speed and drizzle oil in, a little at a time. Season with salt and pepper and set aside.

Carve lamb into 1/4-inch-thick slices (or 0.6 cm).

Toss mesclun with half of the dressing.

To serve, place mesclun on chilled plates and arrange lamb on top. Garnish with peperonata and drizzle with remaining dressing.

Serves 4.

Chef Peter joined Royal Caribbean International in August 2003. Peter was born in Toowoomba, Australia and raised in Asia. He traveled the world and came back to Australia to pursue a culinary apprenticeship, working in several establishments over 3 years and attending COTAH College of Hospitality. He has more than 27 years of hospitality industry experience in Australia, London and Hong Kong with such companies as the Park Royal Group Australia, the Sheraton and Hilton Hotels, the prestigious Savoy Hotel in London and Hamilton Island Resort in the Whitsundays in Queensland, Australia. Peter enjoys getting out his 5.3 meter boat and going cruising with his wife and six children.

2 tablespoons (30 ml) extra virgin olive oil
2 shallots, minced
$1/2$ cup (120 ml) balsamic vinegar

$1/2$ cup (120 ml) extra virgin olive oil
2 tablespoons (30 ml) sherry
1 tablespoon (15 g) honey
$1/3$ cup (90 ml) balsamic vinegar
Salt and freshly ground black
pepper to taste

3 pears
Juice of one lemon
$1/3$ cup (85 g) walnuts
3 tablespoons (45 g) powdered sugar
$1/2$ cup (120 ml) vegetable oil
4 cups (920 g) mesclun mix
1 (4-ounce) (120 g) slice gorgonzola cheese,
cut into small cubes

PEAR AND GORGONZOLA SALAD

For balsamic syrup, warm olive oil in a sauté pan over medium heat and sauté shallots until translucent. Add balsamic vinegar and reduce to a syrup consistency.

For dressing, place olive oil, sherry, honey and balsamic vinegar in a blender. Season to taste and blend until smooth and emulsified. Allow to rest.

Slice pears lengthwise, remove core and sprinkle with lemon juice.

Spray walnuts with water, then toss in sugar. In a small frying pan, heat oil over high heat and fry walnuts for 2 minutes. Drain and place on paper towels.

In a bowl, mix mesclun with 1/4 of the dressing. Toss well.

On chilled plates, arrange the mesclun, sliced pears, cheese, and top with walnuts. Drizzle with balsamic syrup.

Serves 6.

CULINARY NOTES:

Place the gorgonzola in the freezer for 10 minutes prior to cutting. It will be easier and less messy to cube.

Balsamic vinegar is not made with balsam, but is a reference to the fact that it is thick and syrupy. The process of making balsamic vinegar starts by boiling unfermented grape juice to concentrate the flavors. The extract then has Mother of Vinegar added to it and the fermentation process begins. (Mother of Vinegar contains yeasts and Acetobacter bacteria. These bacteria convert the alcohol and sugar into acetic acid or "vinegar.")

The vinegar is then aged for at least 12 years in a series of barrels made from various types of wood including oak, chestnut, mulberry and juniper.

MARINADE

2 cloves garlic, chopped

1 tablespoon (15 g) peeled and
chopped fresh ginger

1 tablespoon (15 g) chopped lemongrass

2 lime leaves, whole

2 tablespoons (30 ml) soy sauce

$1/2$ fresh chili pepper, chopped

$1/2$ tablespoon (7.5 g) green chili paste

1 teaspoon (5 g) sambal olek

$1/4$ cup (60 ml) vegetable oil

5 (6-ounce) (170 g) chicken breasts, skinned

3 tablespoons (45 ml) extra virgin olive oil

2 teaspoons (10 ml) sesame oil

Salt and freshly ground black pepper

PICKLED CUCUMBER

$1/2$ cup (120 ml) white wine vinegar

$1/2$ teaspoon (2.5 g) red crushed pepper

2 tablespoons (30 g) white sugar

1 cucumber, peeled, seeded, and diced

VEGETABLES

2 heads Boston (Bibb) lettuce

1 carrot, julienned

$1/2$ cup (120 g) bean sprouts

1 leek, julienned, white part only

8 green onions

GARNISH

$1/3$ cup (85 g) roasted peanuts,
coarsely chopped

2 limes, quartered

6 red radishes

1 bunch cilantro

Sweet chili sauce, purchased

Peanut sauce, purchased

THAI CHICKEN LETTUCE WRAP

In a bowl, mix all ingredients for marinade. Slice chicken breasts into long, thin strips and marinate in a covered dish for 24 hours in the refrigerator.

In a sauté pan over high heat, warm olive oil. Sauté chicken for 5 minutes or until cooked. Add sesame oil and stir well. Season to taste with salt and black pepper.

For pickled cucumbers, combine first 3 ingredients and bring to a boil. Place cucumbers into a shallow container and pour vinegar mixture over. Cover and refrigerate for at least 1 hour.

Wash and dry lettuce. Place two leaves on each of 6 chilled plates.

Fill lettuce leaves with carrots, bean sprouts, leeks, green onions, and pickled cucumber. Top with sautéed chicken.

Sprinkle with chopped peanuts and garnish each plate with a lime wedge, radish and cilantro.

Serve with ramekins of peanut sauce and sweet chili sauce.

Serves 6.

CULINARY NOTES:

Sambel olek is a hot chile pepper paste used as a table condiment in China and Southeast Asia. It contains chilies, salt, vinegar and sometimes garlic and tamarind.

You can find sambal olek in the imported foods section of your favorite grocery store. If it is not available then you can substitute one minced jalapeño pepper, one teaspoon (5 g) minced garlic and two tablespoons (30 ml) rice vinegar.

BEURRE BLANC

1 shallot, minced
6 black peppercorns, crushed
3/4 cup (175 ml) dry white wine
1 tablespoon (15 ml) freshly squeezed lemon juice
2 tablespoons (30 ml) cider vinegar
1 cup (240 ml) heavy cream
1 pound butter (450 g), room temperature
1 jalapeño pepper, seeded and minced
2 tablespoons (30 g) finely chopped cilantro
Salt and freshly ground black pepper

DRESSING

3/4 cup (175 ml) freshly squeezed orange juice
1 teaspoon (5 g) whole white peppercorns
1 tablespoon (15 g) honey
1 teaspoon (5 g) orange zest
1/2 teaspoon (2.5 g) chopped thyme
1/4 cup (60 ml) extra virgin olive oil
Salt and freshly ground black pepper

VEGETABLES

1 jícama, julienned
2 celery ribs, julienned
2 carrots, julienned
1 orange, segmented
1 tablespoon (15 g) chopped basil

POTATO NESTS

2 large russet potatoes
1 cup (240 ml) vegetable oil, for frying

SCALLOPS

12 sea scallops

GARNISH

Basil leaves, fried

Bartol Cabrera, Executive Chef, CEC

Chef Bartol joined Royal Caribbean International in March 2003. He took on his first chef position for an Italian restaurant in Oberlin, Ohio, attended courses at Cornell University in New York, then moved to Washington, D.C. where he attended Culinary School. While working for the Tai Hotel, he won his first Best Restaurant Award. Bartol also worked for Hilton Hotels and the Waldorf Astoria Hotel in New York City. He began his cruise career on board the QE2 before joining Royal Caribbean International. When not working Bartol enjoys golfing, kayaking and whitewater rafting.

SAUTÉED SCALLOPS IN POTATO NESTS WITH CILANTRO-CHILI BUTTER AND ORANGE-JÍCAMA SALAD

Combine shallots, peppercorns, wine, lemon juice and vinegar in a saucepan. Simmer for 7 minutes until sauce liquids have reduced by two-thirds. Add cream and simmer for 10 minutes. Do not boil. Remove from heat and whisk in butter a little at a time. Strain through a sieve. Adjust seasoning with salt and black pepper. Finish sauce by adding jalapeño and cilantro. Hold the sauce in a bain marie.

For dressing, mix all ingredients except the oil in a non-metal bowl. Slowly whisk in oil a little at a time to emulsify the vinaigrette. Adjust seasoning with salt and black pepper.

In a stainless steel bowl, toss vegetables and half of the vinaigrette. Cover and refrigerate. Just before serving, toss in basil.

Using a mandolin cutter with a waffle grid, slice potatoes very thin and pat dry.

Heat a frying pan over high heat, warm oil and lightly fry potatoes for 10 seconds, remove and let cool on a plate lined with paper towels.

Pat dry and season scallops. Wrap each scallop with one or two wafer potatoes, depending on the size, and fry for 2 to 3 minutes until golden brown.

Place the vegetables on chilled plates, top with scallops and drizzle with butter sauce.

Garnish with fried basil leaves.

Serves 4.

PIZZA DOUGH

2 1/2 teaspoons (1 packet) active dry yeast
1 cup (250 ml) warm water
1 teaspoon (5 g) honey
1 tablespoon (15 ml) extra virgin olive oil
3 cups (700 g) all purpose flour
1 teaspoon (5 g) salt

2 tablespoons (30 ml) extra virgin olive oil

RED ONION JAM

2 tablespoons (30 ml) extra virgin olive oil
1 tablespoon (15 g) butter
10 red onions, peeled and sliced
1/3 cup (60 g) brown sugar
1/3 cup (90 ml) red wine vinegar
Salt and freshly ground black pepper

DUCK CONFIT

2 duck legs confit, purchased

2 cups (500 g) grated mozzarella cheese
2 cups (500 g) grated Fontina cheese
1/4 cup (60 g) grated Parmesan cheese
1 teaspoon (5 g) finely chopped garlic
1 teaspoon (5 g) chopped thyme
2 tablespoons (30 ml) extra virgin olive oil

GARNISH

1 tablespoon (15 ml) extra virgin olive oil
1/4 bunch basil, julienned

RED ONION JAM AND SHREDDED DUCK CONFIT PIZZA

Preheat oven to 500°F or 260°C.

For pizza dough, in a small bowl, dissolve yeast and water. Add honey and stir together. Let sit for 2 minutes or until water is cloudy. Add olive oil and mix well.

Place flour and salt in a food processor fitted with the blade attachment. Pulse a couple times then, with machine running, pour in yeast mixture and process until dough forms a ball. Transfer on lightly floured surface. Knead for 2 minutes adding flour as necessary until dough is smooth and elastic.

Place dough into a lightly oiled bowl. Cover with plastic wrap and let rise for 30 minutes in a warm spot.

Divide dough in 2 to 4 equal pieces. Hand roll into balls and place on a tray. Cover and let rest for 30 minutes.

Place ball on a lightly floured surface. While turning dough, press down on its center then use a rolling pin to get an even circle (8-inches or 20 cm). Form a slightly thicker raised rim around the edge.

Brush pizza with olive oil, avoiding rims. Transfer onto an oiled pizza pan.

For onion jam, heat oil and butter in a large heavy bottom saucepan over low heat and cook onions for 30 minutes, stirring often. Add sugar and vinegar and cook for another 15 minutes or until onion is dark in color and jam-like in consistency. Season with salt and pepper. Allow to cool. Jam can be kept for 1 week once covered and refrigerated.

Remove duck legs from fat, dry with a paper towel and shred.

Sprinkle cheese evenly over crust, top with purple jam, shredded duck and fresh herbs. Drizzle with olive oil.

Bake for 10 minutes or until crust is nicely brown.

To serve, cut pizza into even slices, drizzle with olive oil and finish with basil.

Serves 4.

Johann Petutschnig, Executive Chef, CEC, CCA

Chef Johann began his culinary career in his hometown of Klagenfurt, Austria.

Prior to joining Royal Caribbean International, Johann had the honor of working for the King of Norway. Along the way, he has earned several awards from various international culinary competitions. When Johann joined Royal Caribbean International in July 2005 on board the Navigator of the Seas, he brought with him seven years of shipboard culinary management experience acquired while working with other cruise lines. Among his many professional credentials, he is also an American Culinary Federation certified Executive Chef and Culinary Administrator.

While on vacation, Johann enjoys spending his time fishing in Norway and visiting with his family.

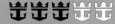

SCALLOPS MARINADE

1/4 cup (60 ml) extra virgin olive oil
1/2 teaspoon (2 g) chili flakes
2 cloves garlic, shaved
1/2 teaspoon (2 g) coriander seeds, roasted and crushed

SCALLOPS

12 large sea scallops
6 skewers

FOCACCIA CROUTONS

1/2 loaf rosemary focaccia, cut into large dice (purchased)
4 tablespoons (60 ml) extra virgin olive oil
Salt and freshly ground black pepper

VINAIGRETTE

2 tablespoons (30 g) Dijon mustard
2 cloves garlic, crushed
Juice of 1 lemon
1/4 cup (60 ml) red wine vinegar
1/2 cup (120 ml) extra virgin olive oil
Salt and freshly ground black pepper

SALAD

6 ripe tomatoes, blanched, peeled, seeded, cut into large dice
1 medium size red bell pepper, cubed
1 medium size green bell pepper, cubed
1 seedless cucumber, cubed
1 medium size red onion, sliced
10 basil leaves
18 kalamata olives
2 tablespoons (30 g) small capers

GARNISH

Mint leaves

PANZANELLA SALAD

Preheat oven to 380°F or 195°C.

For marinade, in a small stainless steel bowl, mix all ingredients, cover and set aside.

Pat dry scallops. Prepare scallop skewers by sliding 2 scallops per skewer. Coat with marinade, cover and refrigerate for 1 hour.

To prepare croutons place diced focaccia on a baking sheet and drizzle with olive oil. Toss well to coat evenly. Season to taste with salt and black pepper. Bake for 5 minutes or until crisp. Set aside to cool on a paper towel.

To grill scallops:

Outdoor grill: Heat to medium high. Brush scallops with the remaining marinade and place on the grill. Cook each slice for 2 minutes, turning only once. Remove from the grill and set aside.

Indoor grill: Lightly oil a grill pan. Set temperature to medium/high heat. Brush scallops with the remaining marinade and place on the pan. Cook each slice for approximately 5 minutes, turning only once. Remove and set aside.

For vinaigrette, place mustard, garlic, lemon, vinegar and olive oil in a blender. Season to taste and blend until smooth and emulsified. Allow to rest.

To make salad, place all ingredients into a large glass bowl, add diced focaccia and 1/2 of the dressing. Mix lightly.

Place salad on chilled plates. Top with scallop skewers and garnish with mint leaves.

Serve remaining dressing on the side.

Serves 6.

CULINARY NOTE:

You can find stainless steel skewers at any department, grocery or kitchen equipment store. They are durable, reusable and easy to clean. If you use bamboo or wooden skewers, try soaking them in water for a few hours first. The moisture will keep them from burning too quickly.

DRESSING

Juice of 1 lemon
1/3 cup (90 ml) red wine vinegar
1 cup (250 ml) extra virgin olive oil
1 tablespoon (15 g) julienned basil
1 teaspoon (5 g) oregano
Salt and freshly ground black pepper

SHRIMP

1 tablespoon (15 g) unsalted butter
1 tablespoon (15 ml) extra virgin olive oil

2 cloves garlic, minced
24 large size shrimp, peeled, deveined and tails left on (size 16/20)
1/4 bunch parsley, finely chopped
Salt and freshly ground black pepper

SALAD

3 heads romaine lettuce, washed, dried and cut crosswise
3 tomatoes, cut in wedges

2 seedless cucumbers, cut in half lengthwise then thickly sliced
3/4 pound (350 g) feta cheese, cubed
1 small red onion, cut in wedges
24 green olives, seeded
24 kalamata olives
1/4 bunch basil, julienned
Salt and freshly ground black pepper

WARM GRILLED SHRIMP GREEK SALAD

For dressing, in a small non-reactive bowl, mix lemon juice and vinegar. Slowly whisk in olive oil. Add herbs and season with salt and black pepper to taste. Cover and refrigerate.

For shrimp, in a cast iron pan over high heat, warm butter and olive oil, add garlic and sauté for 1 minute. Add shrimp and sauté for 4 minutes or until they turn pink. Add parsley and season with salt and black pepper.

To make salad, toss all ingredients with vinaigrette, season to taste and serve in chilled bowls. Crown with shrimp and finish with freshly ground black pepper.

Serves 6.

Our curiosity aroused, we were presented with concepts designed to stimulate the appetite.

APPETIZERS

MARINADE

4 cloves garlic, crushed
1/2 cup (120 ml) extra virgin olive oil
Salt and freshly ground black pepper

GRILLED VEGETABLES

2 Portabella mushrooms, trimmed and
cut into 6 wedges
1 yellow zucchini, trimmed and
cut into 1/2 inch (1.2 cm) slices
1 green zucchini, trimmed and
cut into 1/2 inch (1.2 cm) slices

ROASTED GARLIC

1 head colossal garlic
Extra virgin olive oil
Salt and freshly ground pepper

PESTO

1/2 cup (120 g) pine nuts
3 cups (700 g) loosely packed fresh basil leaves
3 large cloves garlic
1/4 cup (60 g) coarsely grated Parmesan cheese
1 teaspoon (5 g) salt
1 teaspoon (5 g) freshly ground black pepper
2/3 cup (150 ml) extra virgin olive oil

TOMATOES

3 tablespoons (45 ml) extra virgin olive oil
3 tablespoons (45 ml) balsamic vinegar
15 cherry tomatoes

1/2 cantaloupe, sliced into 6 wedges
1/4 pound (120 g) prosciutto, thinly sliced

GARNISH

6 bread sticks of your choice
Frisée lettuce

GRILLED VEGETABLE ANTIPASTI

In a small bowl, mix all ingredients for marinade. Place mushrooms in a small flat dish and pour marinade over. Refrigerate for at least 3 hours. Reserve a little marinade for remaining vegetables.

Preheat oven to 325°F or 165°C.

To roast garlic, cut head into six 1/2-inch-thick slices (1.2 cm). Rub with some oil and season to taste. Place in an ovenproof dish, sprinkle with a little water, and cover with aluminum foil. Roast for 30 minutes or until tender.

For pesto, in a small skillet over high heat, toss pine nuts, taking care not to burn them.

In a food processor, combine garlic, basil, and pine nuts. Process until finely chopped. Add cheese, salt and pepper. With motor on low speed, slowly add olive oil a little at a time, processing until well blended and stopping several times to scrape down the sides.

To grill the vegetables:
Outdoor grill: Heat to medium high. Brush cut sides of vegetables with remaining marinade and place on grill. Cook each slice for 3 to 5 minutes, turning only once. Remove from grill and set aside.

Indoor grill: Lightly oil a grill pan. Set temperature to medium/high heat. Brush cut sides of vegetables with remaining marinade and place on pan. Cook each slice for approximately 5 minutes, turning only once. Remove and set aside.

In a mixing bowl, combine oil and vinegar, add tomatoes, salt and pepper to taste. Toss well.

Wrap cantaloupe with prosciutto.

To serve, arrange grilled vegetables, cantaloupe, balsamic tomatoes, and roasted garlic on chilled plates.

Drizzle with pesto and garnish with bread sticks and bouquet of frisée.

Serves 6.

FILLING

4 (6 to 8-inch)(15-20 cm) sheets rice paper
3/4 pound (350 g) rice noodles

5 tablespoons (75 g) unsalted roasted
cashew nuts
1/3 cup (90 g) julienned mint leaves
1/2 tablespoon (7.5 ml) peanut oil plus 1/3 cup
(90 ml) peanut oil for sautéing
1/4 cup (60 g) shiitake mushrooms

Salt and freshly ground white pepper
1/2 red bell pepper, julienned
1/3 cup (90 g) cilantro leaves
1/3 bunch green onions, finely sliced
1/3 cup (90 g) bean sprouts

GARNISH

Fresh cilantro

SAUCE

1 cup (250 ml) soy sauce
4 tablespoons (60 ml) mirin (rice wine)
1 tablespoon (15 g) sesame seeds

VIETNAMESE VEGETARIAN RICE PAPER ROLL

Soak rice paper in warm water for about 5 minutes, one sheet at a time, wrapping them into individual rolls. This will ensure that they are not over soaked.

Soak noodles in hot water for 10 minutes, then drain.

Coarsely chop cashew nuts and add to drained noodles. Add mint and 1/2 tablespoon (7.5 ml) peanut oil, and mix well.

In a small sauté pan over medium heat, warm remaining peanut oil and sauté mushrooms for 2 minutes. Season with salt and pepper and set aside to cool.

Place soaked rice paper on a tray. Layer mushrooms, noodles, bell pepper, onions, sprouts and 2 cilantro sprigs.

Fold sides in towards the center and roll tightly. To enhance the roll, place a cilantro leaf before finishing rolling the rice paper.

For sauce, combine all the ingredients and serve on the side.

Serves 4.

GARLIC BUTTER

1/2 cup (120 g) butter, softened
1/4 cup (60 g) margarine, softened
3 cloves garlic, minced
1 anchovy fillet, minced
1/2 teaspoon (2 ml) Worcestershire sauce
1/2 teaspoon (2 ml) brandy
3/4 teaspoon (4 ml) freshly squeezed lemon juice
3 tablespoons (45 g) chopped fresh parsley
1 egg yolk
Salt and freshly ground white pepper

GLAZE

1/2 cup (120 g) butter
2 shallots, chopped
2 cloves garlic, chopped
3 tablespoons (45 g) chopped parsley
1/2 teaspoon (2 g) chopped rosemary
1/2 teaspoon (2 g) chopped thyme
1 tablespoon (15 ml) veal demi-glace (page 159)
2 tablespoons (30 ml) red wine
1/2 teaspoon (2 ml) brandy
Salt and freshly ground white pepper

1 (10-ounce) (250 to 300g) can snails

ESCARGOT BOURGUIGNONNE

For garlic butter, combine softened butter and margarine in a food processor and whip continuously, while adding all other ingredients except for the yolk. Continue processing for 3 minutes, until all ingredients are combined and mixture is light and airy. Add the egg yolk and adjust seasoning with salt and pepper. Process for 30 seconds more. Transfer butter mixture to a small bowl and set aside.

Rinse and drain snails, then pat dry.

For glaze, melt butter in a sauté pan over medium heat, and sauté shallots and garlic for 3 minutes. Add herbs, veal demi-glace, red wine and brandy and simmer for 5 to 7 minutes until reduced to a glaze consistency. Add snails and sauté for 2 minutes or until they are heated through. Adjust seasoning with salt and pepper. Remove from heat and let cool.

Preheat oven to 400°F or 200°C.

Transfer snails to snail plate. Cover snails completely with butter mixture.

Bake for 5 minutes or until snails are hot and butter is completely melted and brown on top.

Serve immediately with slices of freshly baked bread.

Serves 4.

CULINARY NOTES:

There are three principal types of edible snails grown in Europe: Petit Gris (Helix Aspersa), Burgundy or Vineyard (Helix Pomatia) and Turkish Edible (Helix Lucorum). The Burgundy snail is the most popular. They grow to be about 1 3/4 inches (4.5 cm) and have a slightly herbal flavor. The Petit Gris is smaller and possesses a fuller, nuttier taste. Petit Gris snails are beginning to be cultivated in the United States partly because they are not as difficult to raise as the Burgundy variety.

FEUILLETÉE

8 (3 1/2 to 4-inch) (7.5 to 10 cm)
squares puff pastry, purchased
1 egg, lightly beaten
2 tablespoons (30 g) poppy seeds
2 tablespoons (30 g) sesame seeds

FILLING

1/2 cup (120 g) butter
2 shallots, chopped
2 cloves garlic, chopped
1/2 cup (120 g) crimini mushrooms, sliced
1/2 cup (120 g) white or button mushrooms, sliced
1/2 cup (120 g) shiitake mushrooms, sliced
1/2 cup (120 g) oyster mushrooms
1 cup (250 ml) white wine
1/4 cup (60 ml) heavy cream
1/4 cup (60 ml) veal demi-glace (page 159)
1 teaspoon (5 g) chopped thyme
Salt and freshly ground black pepper

GARNISH

1/2 red bell pepper, finely diced
1/3 cup chives, finely chopped

WILD MUSHROOM FEUILLETÉE

Preheat oven to 375°F or 190°C.

Grease a baking sheet with butter.

Place pastry squares on baking sheet and brush with beaten egg. Sprinkle, diagonally, half one side with poppy seeds and the other half with sesame seeds. Bake for 15 minutes or until golden and puffed.

In a large sauté pan, over medium heat, melt butter. Add shallots and cook until translucent, about 3 minutes. Add garlic and mushrooms and sauté until liquid is almost evaporated. Season with salt and pepper. Remove mushrooms from pan, leaving the liquid.

Place pan back on the heat, add wine, cream, demi-glace and thyme; simmer for 4 minutes. Return mushrooms to pan and adjust seasoning.

Split pastry squares horizontally into top and bottom halves. Place on warmed plates. Spoon mushroom mixture on each bottom half and cover with top half.

Garnish with bell peppers and chives.

Serves 4.

CULINARY NOTES:

Making puff pastry dough is a rather complex undertaking, and will produce less than satisfactory results if the procedure is not followed exactly.

The good news is there are a number of high quality frozen puff pastry products on the market today that eliminate the need to make a batch at home.

Frozen pastry sheets usually come folded in half and you need to thaw them completely to unfold. If you remove the sheet from the package, slightly spread apart the two halves and place on a baking sheet so it looks like a tent, the sheet will thaw without cracking down the center. This way you will have a complete sheet instead of two broken halves.

Ivo Christoph Jahn, Executive Chef, CEC

Chef Ivo joined Royal Caribbean International in February 2004 as Executive Chef.

Born in Biedenkopf, Germany he began his culinary career in 1986 working for the Waitz Hotel in Frankfurt. He then traveled through Europe working for some of the best Michelin Star restaurants including Traube Tonbach and Domschenke Billerbeck.

In 1999 he completed his Master Chef Certification at the Hotel School in Altötting.

He began his cruise career working for Silver Seas and Celebrity Cruises prior to joining Royal Caribbean International.

When not sailing he enjoys going out with friends, fishing and playing golf.

SALMON MOUSSE

4 ounces (120 g) fresh salmon, skinned and diced
1 egg
$^1/_2$ cup (120 ml) heavy cream
Juice of 1 lemon
Salt and freshly ground white pepper

FISH

3 Dover soles, 1 pound (450 g) each,
skin off, filleted
12 large size shrimp, peeled, deveined, and
tails off (size 16/20)
12 wooden toothpicks
1 tablespoon (15 g) butter
1 shallot, finely diced
$^1/_3$ cup (90 ml) white wine
1 cup (250 ml) fish stock (page 158)

SAUCE

2 tablespoons (30 ml) extra virgin olive oil
2 shallots, finely diced
2 cloves garlic, finely chopped
$^1/_2$ pound (250 g) potatoes, cubed
$^1/_4$ cup (60 g) fresh arugula, cleaned, stems off
$^1/_4$ cup (60 g) fresh spinach, cleaned, stems off
$^1/_4$ cup (60 ml) white wine
1 cup (250 ml) vegetable stock (page 158)
2 tablespoons (30 ml) sour cream
Salt and freshly ground white pepper

GARNISH

1 tablespoon (15 ml) extra virgin olive oil
1 cup (250 g) grape tomatoes
Salt and freshly ground black pepper

DOVER SOLE ROLLS
Arugula-potato sauce and tomato compote

Preheat oven to 300°F or 150°C.

For mousse, place salmon and egg in a blender, run for 3 minutes at medium speed. Slowly add cream, lemon juice, salt and pepper. Beat at medium speed until all ingredients are mixed together, scraping sides occasionally.

Arrange sole fillets on a baking pan, pat dry and spread a thin layer of salmon mousse over each fillet; top with shrimp and roll.

"Close" sole fillets with a toothpick to keep in shape. Set aside.

In a sauté pan over medium heat, melt butter and sauté shallots for 3 minutes until translucent; add wine and fish stock and bring to a boil. Place sole rolls into a 12 inch by 8 inch (30 x 20 cm) baking pan, cover with liquid mixture and bake for 15 minutes.

For sauce, in a sauté pan over medium heat, warm olive oil and sauté shallots and garlic for 3 minutes, add potatoes and sauté for 10 minutes or until potatoes are golden. Add arugula, spinach, white wine and vegetable stock, season to taste and bring to a boil. Reduce heat and simmer for 10 minutes or until potatoes are soft. Place mixture into a blender and blend until smooth. Pass sauce through a sieve and keep warm. Just before serving whisk in sour cream.

In a sauté pan over high heat, warm oil and sauté tomatoes for 2 minutes or until tomatoes burst open. Season with salt and pepper.

Cut sole rolls diagonally. Place rolls in the center of warmed deep plates. Surround with sauce and garnish with tomato compote.

Serves 6.

FISH CAKES

1/2 tablespoon (10 g) coriander, crushed
1 tablespoon (15 ml) sweet chili sauce
2 tablespoons (30 ml) soy sauce
2 tablespoons (30 ml) fish sauce
1 egg
2 pounds (1 kg) halibut or cod, diced small
3 tablespoons (45 ml) vegetable oil
1 tablespoon (15 ml) sesame oil
2 small onions, chopped
1 clove garlic, chopped
1 tablespoon (15 g), peeled chopped ginger
2 tablespoons (30 g) curry paste
1/2 cup (120 g) breadcrumbs
Salt and freshly ground black pepper

SWEET CHILI SAUCE

1/2 cup (120 g) sugar
1 cup (250 ml) water
1 red bell pepper, small diced
3 cloves garlic, minced
1 fresh chili, chopped
1/4 cup (60 ml) soy sauce
1/4 cup (60 ml) fish sauce

GARNISH

2 cucumbers, peeled and julienned
Cilantro sprigs

THAI-STYLE FISH CAKES

In a stainless steel bowl, mix coriander, sweet chili, soy and fish sauce and egg. Mix well and marinate fish, covered and refrigerated, for 1 hour.

Warm 1 tablespoon (15 ml) of vegetable oil and sesame oil and sauté onions in a sauté pan over medium heat for 4 minutes, until translucent. Add garlic and ginger and cook for 1 minute. Do not brown. Stir in curry paste and mix well. Remove from heat and let cool. Stir in fish and transfer mixture into a blender. Blend at medium speed for 2 minutes, until smooth. Transfer into a large bowl and fold in breadcrumbs. Adjust seasoning with salt and pepper. Form into cakes.

For sweet chili sauce, in a saucepan over medium heat, melt sugar in water. Add all ingredients and simmer for about 15 minutes. Remove from heat and transfer to a blender. Blend for 2 minutes until smooth. Place back in saucepan and simmer for another 10 minutes until sauce is thick enough to coat the back of a spoon.

Warm remaining oil over medium-high heat in a sauté pan and cook fish cakes for 2 to 3 minutes on each side.

To serve, arrange cucumber in the center of plates and top with 2 fish cakes. Spoon some chili sauce around, and garnish with cilantro.

Serves 4.

Werner Zimmermann, Executive Chef, CEC

Chef Werner joined the Royal Caribbean International culinary team as an Executive Chef in November 2003.

Born in Hollabrunn, Austria, Werner completed a 3-year professional apprenticeship in the Hotel-Restaurant Marchfelder Hof in Vienna. Werner brings with him years of experience and culinary knowledge working for leading hotels and restaurants in Austria, Switzerland and the Middle East, just to name a few. When not cooking, Werner enjoys riding his Kawasaki ZZR1100 and mountain climbing.

ROASTED PEPPERS
2 bell peppers
2 tablespoons (30 ml) extra virgin olive oil
Salt

MARINADE
2 cloves garlic, minced
Juice of 1/2 lemon
1/3 cup (90 ml) extra virgin olive oil
Salt and freshly ground black pepper
2 tablespoons (30 ml) balsamic vinegar

VEGETABLES
6 portabella caps, stalks and gills removed
12 asparagus, peeled

TAPENADE DRESSING
1/2 cup (120 ml) balsamic vinegar
1 tablespoon (15 g) brown sugar
1 (5-ounce) (150 g) jar chunky black olive tapenade, purchased

TOAST
1/4 cup (60 g) butter, softened and whipped
2 cloves garlic, minced
1 teaspoon (5 ml) fresh lemon juice
1 tablespoon (15 g) grated Parmesan cheese
1 teaspoon (5 g) chopped parsley

1 baguette, sliced
3 1/2 ounces (100 g) goat cheese, softened
Freshly ground black pepper
Fresh thyme

GARNISH
Frisée lettuce

CHAR-GRILLED PORTABELLA CAPS

Preheat oven to 400°F or 200°C.

Place peppers in an ovenproof dish, drizzle with oil, season with salt and roast for 20 minutes or until brown and blistery. Remove peppers from oven, place them into a small bowl and cover with plastic wrap. A small, tightly closed paper bag will also do. This loosens the skins and eases peeling. Peel and cut lengthwise.

For marinade, combine all ingredients in a small stainless steel bowl and mix well. Brush portabella caps with 3/4 of the marinade.

To grill portabella mushrooms, heat a grilling pan over high heat. Sear each side of the mushrooms for approximately 3 minutes or until cooked. Transfer onto a baking sheet, top with roasted pepper strips and remaining marinade. Cover and keep warm.

Blanch asparagus in boiling, salted water for 3 minutes. Cool in ice water, drain and set aside. Reheat in hot water for a few seconds, just prior to serving.

For tapenade dressing, in a small saucepan over medium to low heat, reduce balsamic vinegar and sugar by half. Transfer 3/4 of the glaze into a small stainless steel bowl and let cool. Add olive tapenade and mix well. Cover and refrigerate.

Keep remaining glaze in a small glass bowl to be used for finishing touches.

In a small stainless steel bowl, mix butter, garlic, lemon juice, Parmesan cheese and parsley. Spread butter mixture over slices of baguettes and pan-fry until golden brown turning over once. Spread baguette slices with goat cheese. Sprinkle with pepper and thyme and keep warm.

To serve, place portabella mushrooms in the center of warm appetizer plates, top with asparagus, goat cheese crouton and a bouquet of frisée. Drizzle with tapenade dressing.

Finish with a few drops of balsamic glaze around each plate.

Serves 6.

ASIAN SOY DRESSING

1/4 cup (60 ml) fish sauce

1/2 cup (120 ml) sweet soy sauce

3/4 cup (175 ml) lime juice

1/4 cup (60 ml) vegetable oil

1 cup (250 ml) water

1 tablespoon (15 g) finely chopped ginger

2 cloves garlic, minced

3 tablespoons (45 g) sugar

4 tablespoons (60 g) honey

1 fresh chili, finely chopped

2 tablespoons (30 ml) sesame oil

1 tablespoon (15 g) cornstarch

1 tablespoon (15 g) chopped cilantro

TARTAR

2 pounds (1 kg) yellowfin tuna (Toro A1 sushi grade), small dice

Juice of 2 limes

VEGETABLES

18 pieces small shiitake mushrooms

24 snow peas

1 avocado, peeled, sliced and placed in cold, lemony water

GARNISH

6 ounces (170 g) Alfalfa sprouts

10 red radishes, julienned

1/2 plum tomato, peeled, seeded and julienned

AVOCADO AND YELLOWFIN TUNA TARTAR

For Asian dressing, combine all ingredients with the exception of cilantro and cornstarch. Whisk well. Place 3/4 of the dressing in a stainless steel bowl, cover and refrigerate.

To make sauce, in a small saucepan over medium heat, bring remaining Asian dressing to a boil, add cornstarch a little at a time until sauce coats the spoon. Strain, cover and refrigerate. Upon serving, add cilantro to the sauce.

In a stainless steel bowl, marinate tuna in the cold Asian dressing and lime juice. Cover and refrigerate for 20 minutes.

Sauté mushrooms in a hot saucepan with 2 tablespoons of dressing for 1 minute.

Blanch snow peas in boiling salted water for 2 minutes. Cool in ice water, drain and julienne. Keep refrigerated.

To serve, place tuna tartar in the center of chilled plates. Top with shiitake mushrooms, julienned snow peas and avocado. Finish with Alfalfa sprouts and julienned radishes and tomato.

Drizzle with Asian sauce.

Served on the side, the spiciness of pickled ginger will enhance the taste of the marinated tuna.

Serves 6.

CULINARY NOTES:

Each part of the tuna fish differs in quality, and therefore in price. There are five main cuts to be found on the open market: Otoro, Jutoro, Akami, Belly Cut and Back Cut. Similar to beef sold in the United States, tuna is graded based on the fat content (marbling) found within the meat. Otoro or Toro grade has the highest level of fat and is the most expensive.

ROASTED ZUCCHINI

2 zucchini, cut lengthwise then
in half and scooped out
$^1/4$ cup (60 ml) extra virgin olive oil
Salt and freshly ground black pepper
2 pieces pita bread

BALSAMIC GLAZE

$^1/2$ cup (120 ml) balsamic vinegar

$^1/2$ pound (250 g) red pepper hummus, purchased

GARNISH

$^1/4$ pound (120 g) frisée lettuce
$^1/4$ pound (120 g) lollo rosso lettuce
(baby red leaf)
1 red bell pepper, thinly sliced

FIRE ROASTED RED PEPPER HUMMUS

Preheat oven to 375°F or 190°C.

Season zucchini with salt and pepper, rub with olive oil, and roast in oven for 6 minutes.

In a grilling pan over high heat, mark pita breads, then cut into triangles. Cut 6 triangles per pita.

In a small saucepan over medium heat, reduce balsamic vinegar by half.

Serve the hummus on chilled plates, arrange the lettuce and red bell pepper in the center, place the zucchini on the side, and finish with the pita. Drizzle with the balsamic reduction.

Serves 4.

PINEAPPLE

2 golden pineapples
1/4 cup (60 g) sundried apricots
1 cup (250 g) ricotta cheese
Salt and freshly ground black
pepper to taste

GARNISH

12 pieces sundried apricots
6 mint leaves

SUN-RIPENED PINEAPPLE

Peel pineapples, halved lengthwise, and cut into 2-inch (5 cm) slices.

Chop apricots and mix with ricotta. Season with salt and pepper.

Using 2 tablespoons, form cheese mixture into quenelles – small oval shapes.

On chilled plates, arrange 3 pineapple slices per plate and one quenelle. Garnish with apricot pieces and mint. Finish with freshly ground black pepper.

Serves 6.

PIE

1 pie crust purchased or
1 cup (250 g) all-purpose flour
1/2 teaspoon (5 g) salt
1/4 cup shortening (60 g), room temperature
3 tablespoons (45 ml) water

3 tablespoons (45 ml) extra virgin olive oil
1 cup julienned Vidalia onion (3 large onions)
1 tablespoon (15 g) chopped thyme
Salt and freshly ground black pepper
1/2 cup (120 g) shredded Gruyère cheese

FILLING

3 eggs
1/3 cup (90 ml) heavy cream
1 tablespoon (15 g) chopped parsley
1 tablespoon (15 g) chopped chives
1/2 teaspoon (2 g) ground nutmeg
Salt and freshly ground black pepper

RED PEPPER COULIS

4 red bell peppers
1 tablespoon (15 ml) extra virgin olive oil
Salt and freshly ground black pepper

GARNISH

1 medium Vidalia onion
1/3 cup (90 ml) vegetable oil
Fresh chervil

VIDALIA ONION TART

Preheat oven to 350°F or 180°C.

In a medium bowl, with a fork, lightly stir together flour and salt. With fork, cut shortening into flour until the mixture resembles coarse crumbs. Sprinkle cold water one teaspoon at a time, mixing lightly with fork after each addition, until pastry begins to hold together. With your hands, shape pastry into a ball. Refrigerate for 30 minutes.

On a lightly floured surface, roll pastry in 1/8-inch (0.32 cm) thick circle about 2-inches (5 cm) larger all around than pie mold.

Roll pastry circle gently onto rolling pin. Transfer to pie mold and unroll. With a sharp knife, trim edges, pinch to form a high edge and make a decorative edge by pressing it with a fork. Prick crust with a fork to prevent puffing during baking. Refrigerate for 1/2 hour.

Blind bake pie crust for 7 minutes, remove from oven and let cool.

While crust is baking, warm olive oil in a small saucepan over medium heat, and sauté onions until translucent, about 4 minutes. Add thyme and season with salt and pepper.

Spread onions evenly in pie crust. Sprinkle with cheese.

In a medium bowl beat eggs lightly, add cream, fresh herbs and seasonings. Beat until well mixed.

Pour mixture over cheese and onions. Bake for 40 minutes.

For coulis, blanch peppers in boiling water for 5 minutes. Cool in ice water, and remove skins.

In a blender, purée the peppers and olive oil until smooth. Season with salt and pepper.

For garnish, in a small skillet over high heat, warm oil and deep fry onion until golden brown, about 2 minutes.

Serve slices of tart on warmed plates, top with fried onions, and garnish with spoons of pepper coulis.

Serves 6.

CULINARY NOTES:

Vidalia onions thrive in the sandy soil and mild conditions found in southeastern Georgia. Nowhere else on earth can a Vidalia onion be grown that will produce the same sweetness for which this onion is so famous. Several attempts have been made to cultivate it in other parts of the country, but the results have always been the same; hot, not sweet.

The evening's culinary compositions, in harmony with artistic representations, were layered with subtlety.

SOUPS/ BREADS

SUGAR SYRUP
1/4 cup (60 g) sugar
1/4 cup (60 ml) water

CHILLED SOUP
1 cup (250 ml) freshly squeezed orange juice
1/4 cup (60 g) fresh or frozen blueberries
1/4 cup (60 g) fresh or frozen strawberries
1/4 cup (60 g) fresh or frozen raspberries
1 shot crème de cassis liqueur
1/4 cup (60 ml) club soda
1/2 cup (120 ml) buttermilk

CHILLED FOREST BERRY AND BUTTERMILK SOUP

In a small saucepan, mix sugar and water over medium heat and simmer until sugar is dissolved. Cover and refrigerate.

In a food processor, blend juice and berries. Adjust sweetness by adding sugar syrup as needed. Add crème de cassis.

Just before serving, add club soda to give the soup a sparkling twist.

Serve in chilled soup bowls and finish with a swirl of buttermilk.

Serves 6.

CULINARY NOTES:

The most complicated step in this recipe is making the sugar syrup. Don't let the sugar and water mixture boil, as the sugar will start to caramelize. Once cooled the sugar syrup can be stored in a plastic bottle for several days for use in a variety of other recipes and bar mixes.

CHILLED SOUP

3 pounds (1.4 kg) ripe bananas
1¹/₄ cup (300 ml) freshly squeezed orange juice
1 cup (250 ml) freshly squeezed lime juice
¹/₄ cup (60 ml) canned coconut milk
¹/₄ cup (60 ml) heavy whipping cream
1¹/₄ cup (300 g) plain yogurt
1 shot banana liqueur

GARNISH

24 orange segments
Fresh basil leaves

CHILLED ORANGE AND BANANA SOUP

In a food processor blend bananas with juices, coconut milk, cream, and yogurt. If the mixture is too thick, add more orange juice as needed.

Add banana liqueur and blend thoroughly.

Serve in chilled soup bowls. Garnish with orange segments and basil.

Serves 6.

CULINARY NOTES:

Segmenting an orange is simply removing the flesh of the fruit from the skin and pith.

With a sharp knife, completely remove the skin and as much of the white pith as possible. Look for the white ribs separating each segment and run the blade of the knife between the rib and the segment. Repeat on both sides and the segment will fall free from the ribs.

SOUP

1 tablespoon (15 g) butter
1/3 pound (150 g) bacon, chopped
2 cloves garlic, chopped
2 Spanish onions, finely diced
4 stalks celery, finely diced
3 tablespoons (45 g) all-purpose flour
1 1/2 quarts (1.5 L) fish stock (page 158)
1/2 pound (250 g) potatoes cut into
1/2-inch (1.2 cm) dice

1/2 pound (250 g) crabmeat
16 pieces medium shrimp, raw, peeled
and deveined
1 1/4 cups (300 ml) milk
1/3 cup (90 ml) heavy cream
Salt and freshly ground white pepper

GARNISH

Fresh parsley or dill, chopped

SHEE CRAB SOUP

In a large saucepan or small stockpot melt butter and cook bacon for 5 minutes over low heat. Add garlic, onion, and celery, and sauté for about 4 minutes or until onion is soft and translucent. Do not brown.

Gradually add flour, stirring to create a roux. Cook over medium heat for 3 to 4 minutes. Do not brown. Slowly whisk in stock. Bring to a boil and stir constantly to dissolve lumps. Add potatoes and simmer until they are tender.

Stir in crabmeat, shrimp, milk, and cream.

Season to taste with salt and pepper. Bring soup to a simmer.

Ladle the soup into individual soup bowls. Garnish with herbs.

Serves 6.

CHILLED SOUP

2 medium tomatoes
2 red bell peppers
4 tablespoons (60 ml) extra virgin olive oil
2 shallots, finely chopped
8 ounces (230 g) canned pimentos
1 slice white bread, crumbled
$1/2$ tablespoon (10 ml) balsamic vinegar
3 cups (700 ml) tomato juice
Salt and freshly ground black pepper

SCALLOPS

6 jumbo scallops
1 tablespoon (15 ml) virgin olive oil
Salt and freshly ground black pepper

AVOCADO TOWER

2 avocados, peeled and chopped
Juice of 1 lemon

GARNISH

$1/4$ bunch basil, finely julienned

ZUPPA FREDDA AI POMODORI E PEPERONI DOLCI CON CAPESANTE ED AVOCADO

Chilled Red Bell Pepper Soup and Avocado Tartar

Preheat oven to 350°F or 180°C.

Fill a small pan with water and bring to a boil. Using a sharp knife, gently tear the skin of the tomatoes lengthwise in a couple of spots and place in the boiling water for about 3 minutes. Place tomatoes in ice water for 2 minutes or until the skin starts separating from the tomato. Peel, cut in half and take off seeds using a small spoon. Slice and dice tomatoes.

Place the red peppers in an ovenproof dish, drizzle with 2 tablespoons (30 ml) of olive oil. Roast for 20 minutes or until brown and blistery. Remove peppers from oven. Place them into a small bowl and cover with plastic wrap. A small, tightly closed paper bag will do also. This loosens the skins and eases peeling. Peel and finely dice the peppers.

In a large pan over medium heat, warm remaining olive oil; add shallots and sauté for about 3 minutes or until shallots are tender and translucent. Add pimentos and sauté for 3 minutes. Add bread crumbs, vinegar, tomatoes and tomato juice. Transfer into a blender, including roasted peppers, and blend until smooth. Adjust seasoning with salt and pepper. Cover and refrigerate for 2 hours.

Pat dry and season sea scallops. In a saucepan, over medium heat, warm oil and sauté scallops until firm and opaque, about two minutes on each side.

Peel and dice avocados. Mix with lemon juice.

Using a biscuit cutter or small round cookie cutter as a mold, tightly pack avocado in, being careful not to mash it.

Remove mold and pour an equal amount of soup in each bowl (a soup or pasta bowl may be used). Top each avocado "tower" with a sautéed jumbo scallop. Garnish each tower with julienned basil.

Serves 6.

CULINARY NOTES

Fresh scallops perish quickly when out of water, so you will most likely find them already shucked. If you come across scallops that are still in the shell, buy those as they are sure to be the freshest. When shopping for scallops, look for a pearly off-white or pale-golden color. Bright-white scallops have been treated with chemicals to preserve freshness. Avoid! Scallops should also have a fresh, sweet smell. Spoiled scallops smell like sulfur.

SOUP

2 cups (500 g) white cannellini beans
1/2 cup (120 g) pearled barley

2 tablespoons (30 ml) extra virgin olive oil
1/4 cup (60 g) chopped celery
1/4 cup (60 g) chopped carrots
1 yellow onion, diced
2 cloves garlic, chopped

1 ounce (30 g) prosciutto, small dice
1 ounce (30 g) pancetta, small dice
1 slice bacon, diced
1/4 cup (60 ml) dry white wine
1 - 16 ounce (450 g) can of chopped tomato
8 cups (2 L) chicken stock (page 158)
2 each rosemary sprigs
Salt and freshly ground black pepper

GARNISH

1 plum tomato, seeded and sliced
12 Parmesan shavings
1/4 bunch Italian parsley, finely chopped
1 tablespoon (15 ml) extra virgin olive oil

ZUPPA GRAN FARO

Soak cannellini beans and pearled barley in separate glass bowls filled with cold water, overnight.

In a large saucepan or medium size stockpot, over medium heat, warm oil and sauté vegetables and garlic for 10 minutes or until lightly caramelized.

Add prosciutto, pancetta and bacon and sauté until crisp. Deglaze with white wine.

Drain cannellini beans and add to vegetable mixture. Stir in canned tomatoes and chicken stock. Add rosemary and season with salt and pepper. Bring to a boil, reduce heat and simmer for 40 minutes or until beans are tender.

In a small pan filled with salted hot water, cook barley until al dente or about 15 minutes. Strain and set aside.

Remove half of the beans from soup.

Transfer soup into a blender and blend until smooth, adding some of the reserved beans a little at a time until a thickened, chunky consistency is achieved. Adjust seasoning with salt and pepper.

Place 1 tablespoon (15g) of barley and 1 tablespoon (15 g) of beans into warmed soup bowls. Garnish with sliced tomato, Parmesan shavings and parsley.

Ladle soup into individual serving bowls. Drizzle with olive oil and sprinkle with freshly ground black pepper.

Serves 6.

CULINARY NOTES:

Pancetta is the Italian word for bacon. It is pork that has been salt-cured and spiced, and dried for 3 months (but is usually not smoked). Pancetta can be found in most delicatessen and large supermarkets.

American bacon may be substituted. However, try to find bacon that is not smoked as it will add a different flavor profile to the finished dish.

1 quart (1 L) chicken stock (page 158)
1 tablespoon (15 g) peeled and chopped ginger
1 tablespoon (15 g) chopped lemongrass
1/2 pound (250 g) chicken breast, cut into
1/2-inch (1.2 cm) strips

3/4 cup (150 g) rice noodles

(page 158)

VEGETABLES

1 tablespoon (15 g) peeled and chopped ginger
3/4 cup (150 g) shiitake mushrooms, julienned
1/2 cup (120 g) julienned scallions
1/2 cup (120 g) julienned leeks
1/2 cup (120 g) carrots, julienned
1/2 cup (120 g) soybean sprouts

GARNISH

2 tablespoons (30 g) peeled and julienned ginger
1/4 bunch cilantro

SAIGON CHICKEN NOODLE SOUP

Simmer chicken broth with chopped ginger, lemongrass and chicken strips for 20 minutes.

Soak rice noodles in hot water for 10 minutes, then drain. Cool down immediately in ice water. Drain and set aside.

Place all vegetables in a colander and simmer for 3 to 4 minutes in the hot chicken broth. Reheat rice noodles the same way.

Divide chicken, vegetables, and noodles among individual soup bowls, then ladle the broth. Garnish with ginger and cilantro.

Serves 6.

CULINARY NOTES:

Blanching is a cooking term that actually has a number of different meanings. In this case blanching is the partial-cooking of food items (usually vegetables) in order to make them tender without cooking out all the color and texture. By placing the vegetables in boiling water for a short period of time, they begin to cook. Shocking in ice water immediately stops the cooking process, thus preserving their colors, firmness and freshness.

SPICE PASTE

4 dried red chilies, seeded and chopped
1 medium red onion, chopped
1 teaspoon (5 g) peeled and chopped ginger
4 stems lemongrass, white part only, sliced
2 fresh red chilies, seeded and chopped
10 macadamia nuts
2 teaspoons (10 g) shrimp paste
2 tablespoons (30 g) turmeric
2 tablespoons (30 ml) vegetable oil

PRAWN SOUP

1 pound (500 g) prawn, head on, shell on
1 1/2 quarts (1.5 L) water
1 tablespoon (15 ml) vegetable oil
2 cups (500 ml) coconut milk
8 fish balls, purchased from an Asian market
1 pound (500 g) rice noodles

GARNISH

1 cucumber, peeled, seeded and julienned
1/2 cup (120 g) bean sprouts

PRAWN LAKSA

Nethaji Dasarathan, Executive Chef, CEC

Chef Nethaji joined Royal Caribbean International in 1989 and has served on many of the company's ships since. Nethaji was born in Madras and studied for 3 years in India where he achieved a Diploma in Catering Technology. He worked as a senior Chef de Partie for the Sheraton Hotel in India for 4 years. During his spare time, he likes photography, traveling and trying different types of cuisine.

To make the paste, soak chilies in hot water for 20 minutes. Place all paste ingredients in a blender and blend for 3 minutes, until very smooth, scraping the bowl regularly.

For prawn stock, set aside 4 prawns, then peel and devein remainder, reserving heads and shells. Sauté heads and shells in a deep pan over medium heat for 5 minutes until shells and heads become deep orange and aromatic. Stir in 1 cup (250 ml) of the water and boil until water has almost evaporated. Add another cup (250 ml) of water, bring to a boil and reduce by half before adding remaining water. Bring stock to a boil and simmer for 30 minutes. In a small saucepan, cook reserved prawns with a little stock, simmering for 3 to 4 minutes, or until shrimp are pink.

Heat oil in a wok or sauté pan and cook spice paste over low heat for about 8 minutes, stirring occasionally until very aromatic. Stir in prawn stock and coconut milk. Bring to a boil, then lower the heat and simmer for 10 minutes. Add peeled prawns and sliced fish balls and simmer for another 5 minutes.

Warm reserved prawns with a little stock.

In a separate pan with boiling water, cook the noodles for 5 minutes. Drain well and serve in deep soup bowls.

Ladle the soup, prawns and fish balls over the noodles. Garnish with the cucumber and bean sprouts, and top each bowl with one of the reserved prawns.

Serves 4.

2 (1/4-ounce or 7 g) packages dry yeast
1 tablespoon (15 g) sugar
1 cup (250 ml) water, lukewarm
2 pounds (900 g) all-purpose flour
1/4 teaspoon (1.2 g) salt
1/2 cup (120 ml) milk
4 eggs
1/2 cup (120 g) butter, room temperature
1 teaspoon (5 ml) vanilla extract

Zest of 1/2 lemon
2 tablespoons (30 ml) rum
1/2 cup (120 g) raisins
1/2 cup (120 g) dried cranberries

1 egg yolk, beaten

GARNISH
Slivered almonds

AUSTRIAN STRIEZEL

Preheat oven to 400°F or 200°C.

To prepare dough, combine yeast, sugar and 1/2 cup (120 ml) water in a bowl and whisk until yeast has dissolved. In a stand mixer or a large bowl, combine all ingredients except raisins and cranberries and mix for 2 minutes at low speed, then for 8 minutes at high speed using a dough hook. The dough should be soft and elastic.

If kneading by hand, add flour a cup (250 g) at a time, and knead for 10 minutes. Add raisins and cranberries to dough and mix well. Shape dough into a ball.

Cover and set aside in a warm, draft-free place for 20 minutes.

Punch down dough and divide into 1 pound (450 g) loaves. Cover and allow to relax for 20 minutes.

Cut dough into 3 equal pieces and hand roll each dough into a 12-inch by 4-inch strip (30 x 10 cm).

Line a baking sheet with parchment paper, and spray with nonstick spray. Transfer rolls to the baking sheet and braid, tucking the ends under. Cover and let rise for 20 minutes.

Brush braids with egg yolk and let rise for another 10 minutes. Brush a second time and sprinkle with slivered almonds.

Bake for 20 minutes, until nicely golden or until loaves sound hollow when their undersides are thumped.

Serves 6.

Robert Heindl, Bakery Supervisor

Chef Robert joined Royal Caribbean International in August 2002. Robert was born in the Austrian capital of Vienna, then moved to the small Austrian village of Deutschkreutz. It was there that Robert ventured into the baking industry, gaining classical training in traditional handmade European-style bread-making techniques. Robert was enticed to join the cruise ship industry at the age of 20, taking him around the world many times over on the world famous QE2. When not baking, Robert enjoys mountain biking.

WINDJAMMER

CHOPS GRILLE

Portofino

JADE

Our adventure was enhanced with continual anticipation of each new course.

PASTA

1 1/2 pounds (800 g) cheese tortellini, purchased

SAUCE
1/3 cup (100 g) blue cheese, crumbled
1/2 cup (120 ml) heavy cream
1/3 cup (100 g) julienned sundried tomatoes
Salt and freshly ground white pepper

GARNISH
1/3 cup (100 g) blue cheese, crumbled
1/3 bunch chive sprigs

CHEESE TORTELLINI

WINE PAIRING – ▼ – VEUVE CLICQUOT PONSARDIN, BRUT, FRANCE

Cook tortellini in a stockpot of boiling salted water until al dente, about 8 minutes. Drain well.

Meanwhile, in a small saucepan over low heat, melt blue cheese in heavy cream. Simmer for about 7 minutes, until the sauce has reduced by half.

Toss tortellini with blue cheese mixture and sundried tomatoes. Season with salt and pepper.

Serve on warmed plates. Sprinkle with blue cheese and garnish with chive sprigs.

Serves 4.

CULINARY NOTES:

Tortellini is derived from the Italian word for "cake." As legend has it the shape of this pasta is supposed to be representative of the navel of the Goddess Venus.

Al dente in Italian means "to the tooth." It refers to pasta that is cooked through but still offers some resistance when bitten.

PASTA DOUGH

3 cups (700 g) flour
8 egg yolks
1 teaspoon (5 g) salt
1 teaspoon (5 ml) extra virgin olive oil
2 to 3 tablespoons (30 to 45 ml) water
(as needed)

Semolina or all purpose flour for dusting

SAUCE

1 tablespoon (15 ml) extra virgin olive oil
3 tablespoons (45 g) butter
1 shallot, finely chopped
1/4 cup (60 ml) Grey Goose vodka
1/2 cup (120 ml) fish stock (page 158)
1/2 cup (120 ml) heavy cream
Salt and freshly ground white pepper

8 ounces (250 g) smoked salmon,
cut in thin strips

GARNISH
Dill sprigs

FRESH PASTA IN VODKA, CAVIAR AND SMOKED SALMON CREAM SAUCE

Joachim Moeller, Executive Chef, CEC

Chef Joachim of Austria comes to us with over sixteen years of professional culinary and management experience.

He started his training in a family-owned restaurant in Lake Edersee, Germany, then went to work for various top Michelin Star-rated restaurants, as well as the Radisson Corporation.

His first foreign destination was London, England, where he joined the Radisson Edwardian Hotel culinary team.

As an Executive Chef on board the Royal Caribbean International ships, Joachim is in charge of coaching, training, and directing more than 150 cooks in order to serve more than 2,000 guests every day.

When not on board, Joachim enjoys spending time riding around Europe on his Harley Davidson® and traveling abroad.

For pasta, in a food processor fitted with a steel blade, combine flour, egg yolks, salt, oil and 2 tablespoons (30 ml) water. Process at medium speed until dough holds together. Pinch dough to test it. If it's too dry, add 1 more tablespoon (15 ml) of water and process until it forms a moist ball.

Place dough onto a lightly floured surface and hand knead into a smooth ball.

Wrap in plastic and let rest at room temperature for 1 hour.

To roll out dough using a pasta roller, cut dough into four equal pieces. Set roller at widest opening. Flatten first piece of dough into a thick strip. Dust pasta roller and run pasta through the machine, one at a time. Process dough through roller 2 to 3 more times until dough is smooth and somewhat elastic. Repeat operation twice using smaller openings each time.

To roll out dough by hand, cut dough into 8 equal pieces. Roll each ball under palm for 1 minute. Place ball on a lightly

floured flat surface. While turning the dough, hand press down on its center. Use a rolling pin to get a rectangular dough shape. Repeat operation as many times as necessary until dough is thin and elastic.

Cut and roll pasta as desired.

For sauce, in a heavy saucepan over medium heat, warm oil and 1 tablespoon (15 g) of butter, and sauté shallot until translucent, about 3 minutes. Deglaze with vodka and reduce by half. Add fish stock and simmer for 2 minutes. Add heavy cream, season to taste with salt and pepper and simmer for 10 minutes. Do not boil. Remove from heat and whisk in remaining butter a little at a time.

While sauce is simmering, cook pasta in a stockpot of boiling salted water until al dente. Drain well and toss with olive oil.

Add smoked salmon and pasta to sauce. Toss to coat, arrange into warmed serving bowls and garnish with dill.

Serves 6.

SAUCE

2 tablespoons (30 ml) extra virgin olive oil
2 shallots, chopped
1 clove garlic, chopped
1/2 red bell pepper, chopped
1 poblano chili, seeded and finely chopped
4 ounces (120 g) coppa (smoked pork), diced
1/4 cup (60 ml) vegetable stock (page 158)
1 cup (250 g) spinach
Salt and freshly ground black pepper

PASTA

1 pound (450 g) dry tagliatelli pasta
1 teaspoon (5 ml) extra virgin olive oil

GARNISH

Grated Parmesan cheese

TAGLIATELLI CON COPPA

Cook tagliatelli in a stockpot of boiling salted water until al dente, about 6 to 8 minutes. Drain well and toss with olive oil.

To make sauce, warm oil and sauté shallots in a saucepan over medium heat for 3 minutes, until translucent. Add garlic and cook for 1 minute. Do not brown. Add peppers, chile and coppa and cook for 2 minutes. Moisten with vegetable stock and add spinach. Adjust seasoning and cook for another 2 minutes until spinach is wilted.

Add pasta to sauce, toss and cook for a couple minutes until pasta is heated through. Serve in deep bowls and finish with Parmesan cheese.

Serves 4.

Martin Grabenhoffer, Executive Chef, CEC

Chef Martin, a native of Graz, Austria, joined Royal Caribbean International in 2000. He took a keen interest in cooking at an early age, assisting his mother with her apple strudel which was a local legend. Martin followed his passion for cooking, attaining a degree in hospitality and studying at Austria's prestigious Institute of Hotel Management and Catering in Bad Gleichenberg. He began his career with the KD Riverline in Germany, eventually becoming their Corporate Executive Chef. Martin expanded his knowledge of international cuisines, traveling to destinations such as Rapperswil, Venice and the Canary Islands. Martin was involved with the world trade exhibition Expo 2000 in Hannover and has worked aboard the QE2. When not working, Martin likes to garden, scuba dive and listen to classical music.

1 tablespoon (15 ml) extra virgin olive oil
1 tablespoon (15 g) butter
1 shallot, finely chopped
1 clove garlic, chopped
1/4 cup (60 g) crimini mushrooms, sliced
1/4 cup (60 g) white or button mushrooms, sliced
1/4 cup (60 g) shiitake mushrooms, sliced
1/4 cup (60 g) oyster mushrooms
1 tablespoon (15 g) all-purpose flour
1/4 cup (60 ml) dry white wine
1/2 cup (120 ml) vegetable stock (page 158)

3/4 cup (175 ml) heavy cream
Salt and freshly ground black pepper
1 teaspoon (5 g) ground nutmeg
1 teaspoon (5 g) chopped thyme
2 tablespoons (30 g) grated Parmesan cheese
1 teaspoon (5 ml) white truffle oil

1 pound (450 g) dry linguini pasta
1 teaspoon (5 ml) extra virgin olive oil

GARNISH
1/4 bunch thyme

TRUFFLED WILD MUSHROOM LINGUINI ALFREDO

In a heavy saucepan over medium heat, warm oil and butter, and sauté shallots until translucent, about 3 minutes, add garlic and sauté for 1 minute; do not brown. Add mushrooms and sauté for 2 minutes. Remove mushrooms but leave liquid in the pan. Return pan to burner, stir in flour, add white wine and reduce by half. Add stock and heavy cream, season with salt, pepper and nutmeg. Simmer for 10 minutes. Return mushrooms to pan, adjust seasoning, and heat through. Keep warm. At the last minute, toss in thyme, Parmesan, and truffle oil.

While sauce is simmering, cook linguini in a stockpot of boiling salted water until al dente, about 6 to 8 minutes. Drain well and toss with olive oil.

Add pasta to sauce. Toss to coat and serve immediately. Garnish with thyme.

Serves 4.

CULINARY NOTES:

A truffle is a wild fungus and a cousin of the mushroom. Truffles have been referred to as "the diamond of the kitchen" because of their high price, relative rarity and difficulty in cultivating.

Truffle oil is an inexpensive alternative to fresh truffles as they impart the same flavor without the added expense.

UDON NOODLES

1 pound (450 g) Udon Japanese noodles

SHRIMP

1 tablespoon (15 ml) extra virgin olive oil
18 large size shrimp, peeled, deveined, and tail on (size 16/20)
1/4 cup (60 ml) fish stock (page 158)
Salt and freshly ground black pepper

SAUCE

1 tablespoon (15 ml) extra virgin olive oil
1 small Vidalia onion, finely diced
1 cucumber, peeled, seeded and diced
2 plum tomatoes, blanched, peeled, seeded and diced
1/4 cup (60 ml) Martini & Rossi® Bianco
1/2 bunch basil, finely chopped
1/2 bunch cilantro, finely chopped
1/2 bunch chives, finely chopped
Juice of 2 lemons
2 tablespoons (30 ml) apple cider vinegar
Salt and freshly ground white pepper

GARNISH

Cilantro sprigs

SHRIMP UDON

Markus Zihlmann, Executive Chef, CEC

Chef Markus was born and raised in Switzerland. There he attended culinary school and later trained in some of the most renowned 5 star hotels, alternating positions between summer and winter resorts.

He roamed the world working in Germany, France, New Zealand and finally Australia, where he settled with his wife and two daughters.

His great zeal for food led him to open his own restaurant in Melbourne. But his love of travel pushed him to look for something different. Working for Royal Caribbean International finally allowed him to combine his love for food and travel.

When not on board, Markus enjoys spending time with his family. He also loves experimenting with local flavors and has developed a passion for seafood and fish dishes.

Cook Udon noodles in a stockpot filled with boiling water for 5 minutes or until noodles are tender. Drain and soak noodles in ice water for 2 minutes or until cold. Drain and set aside.

To prepare shrimp, in a sauté pan over high heat, warm oil and sauté shrimp for 5 minutes or until they turn pink. Add fish stock, season with salt and pepper and bring to a boil. Cover and keep warm on side of stove.

For sauce, in a sauté pan over medium heat, warm olive oil and sauté onion for 4 minutes or until translucent. Do not brown. Add cucumbers and tomatoes and sauté for 2 minutes. Deglaze with Martini & Rossi® Bianco, add herbs, lemon juice and vinegar. Bring to a boil and simmer for 3 minutes. Adjust seasoning with salt and pepper.

Add pasta to sauce; toss and cook for 3 minutes or until pasta is heated through.

Serve in warmed, deep bowls and top with shrimp. Finish with fresh cilantro sprigs.

Serves 6.

4 (6-ounce) (170 g) halibut steaks

MARINADE
Juice of 2 lemons
2 cloves garlic, chopped
1/4 cup (60 ml) extra virgin olive oil
Salt and freshly ground black pepper

SAUCE
2 tablespoons (30 ml) vegetable oil
2 cloves garlic, chopped
2 tablespoons (30 g) Dijon mustard
2 tablespoons (30 g) all-purpose flour
1/4 cup (60 g) julienned sundried tomatoes
1 teaspoon (5 g) Cajun spice

1/4 teaspoon (1 g) paprika
1/4 teaspoon (1 ml) Tabasco® sauce
1 teaspoon (5 ml) Worcestershire sauce
Juice of 1 lime
1 cup (250 ml) chicken stock, warm (page 158)
1/2 cup (120 ml) heavy cream
Salt and freshly ground black pepper

PASTA
1 pound (450 g) dry linguini pasta
1 teaspoon (5 ml) extra virgin olive oil

GARNISH
Chopped parsley

CAJUN LINGUINI

Prepare marinade in a stainless steel bowl by combining all ingredients. Coat the fish with marinade, cover and refrigerate for 1 hour.

For sauce, in a saucepan over medium heat, warm oil and sauté garlic for 1 minute until fragrant. Add mustard and flour, and stir. Add sundried tomatoes, spices, Tabasco®, Worcestershire sauce and lime juice, and mix well. Slowly incorporate chicken stock a little at a time. Bring to a boil and simmer for 10 minutes. Add cream and adjust seasoning with salt and pepper. Simmer for about 7 minutes, until sauce is thick enough to coat the back of a spoon. Do not boil. Keep warm.

While sauce is simmering, cook the linguini in a stockpot of boiling salted water until al dente, about 6 to 8 minutes. Drain well and toss with the olive oil.

In a grilling pan over high heat, sear halibut steaks for 1 minute on each side, then reduce heat to medium and finish cooking for about 6 minutes or until fish is firm and opaque at the center when pierced with the tip of a small knife.

Toss pasta with sauce and place into warmed deep plates. Top with fish and finish with parsley.

Serves 4.

Stephen Yates, Senior Executive Chef, CEC

Chef Stephen joined Royal Caribbean in January 2001. He is originally from Canada. Stephen began his culinary career at 15, working in the kitchens of the Toronto Four Seasons. Stephen has had the opportunity to work in some of the finest hotels and resorts Canada has to offer, including Chateau Whistler, Château Frontenac and Banff Springs. When not on board, Stephen enjoys reading and experiencing world cuisine.

LOBSTER STOCK

3 (5 to 6-ounce) (150-170 g) Maine lobster tails
1 tablespoon (15 g) unsalted butter
1 shallot, finely diced
1 small yellow onion, finely diced
1 clove garlic, chopped
Shells of the lobster tails
1/4 cup (60 ml) brandy
1 large tomato, peeled, seeded and diced
1 tablespoon (15 g) tomato paste
2 tablespoons (30 g) all-purpose flour
3/4 cup (175 ml) fish stock, warmed (page 158)
1 teaspoon (5 g) chopped tarragon
1/4 teaspoon (1.2 g) chopped thyme
Salt and freshly ground black pepper

LOBSTER SAUCE

1 tablespoon (15 g) butter
12 pieces large shrimp, raw, peeled,
and deveined
1/3 cup (90 ml) dry white wine
Salt and freshly ground white pepper
1/3 bunch basil, julienned
1/3 cup (90 ml) heavy cream, loosely whipped

PASTA

1 pound (450 g) dry spaghetti pasta
1 teaspoon (5 ml) extra virgin olive oil

VEGETABLES

1/3 pound (150 g) baby squash
1/3 pound (150 g) patty pan squash
1/3 cup (90 g) green peas

GARNISH

Basil leaves

SPAGHETTINI ALL'ARAGOSTA E MAZZANCOLLE
Prawns and Lobster Spaghetti in Lobster Cream Sauce

To prepare lobster stock, steam lobster tails for 5 minutes, remove and let cool. Separate meat from the shells and slice 1/2-inch (1.2 cm) thick. Set aside.

In a saucepan over medium heat, melt butter and sauté shallot and onion for 4 minutes, until translucent. Add garlic and sauté for a few seconds. Add lobster shells, stir for a few seconds and moisten with brandy. Stir in tomato, and tomato paste, and simmer for 5 minutes. Add flour, stirring until it has disappeared. Add fish stock a little at a time, stirring between each addition, to dissolve lumps. Add herbs and simmer for 20 to 25 minutes. Strain through a fine sieve.

For lobster sauce, in a small saucepan over medium heat, melt butter and sauté shrimp and lobster for 1 minute. Add white wine, season with salt and pepper, add lobster stock and simmer for 5 minutes. Do not boil.

Cook spaghetti in a stockpot of boiling salted water until al dente, about 6 to 8 minutes. Drain well and toss with olive oil.

Blanch vegetables for 2 minutes, then cool in ice water and drain well. Set aside.

At the last minute, stir basil and cream into sauce to create a froth, and gently toss pasta with sauce.

Serve on warmed plates and garnish with basil leaves.

Serves 4.

CULINARY NOTES:

Lobsters are best if purchased while they are still alive. A live lobster should have a hard, dark-red or black shell and display a lot of movement both in and out of the water. Lobsters curl their tails under their body when picked up.

Lobsters should be prepared immediately but will keep fresh in the refrigerator for 2 days if wrapped in damp newspaper punched with holes.

Shrimp are customarily packaged for sale based on count or the number of individual headless, shell-on shrimp in a pound. "10 and under" means ten or less shrimp per pound, "10-15" yields between 10 and 15 shrimp per pound. You should not purchase shrimp by their names, e.g. jumbo, large, or medium.

The chefs were masters at enhancing the delicate flavors of seafood with international flair.

FISH AND SEAFOOD

FRUIT SALSA

3 firm mangoes, peeled and julienned

1 firm small papaya, peeled and julienned

2 pink grapefruits, segmented and halved lengthwise

2 oranges, peeled and segmented (reserve orange ribs for citrus butter)

2 limes, peeled and segmented

Juice of 1 orange

Juice of 1 lime

$^1/_4$ bunch chives, finely chopped

$^1/_4$ bunch cilantro leaves

FISH

$^1/_2$ cup (120 g) Japanese breadcrumbs

$^1/_2$ bunch parsley, finely chopped

$^1/_4$ bunch thyme, finely chopped

6 (6-ounce) (170 g) Alaskan halibut steaks

Juice of 1 lemon

Salt and freshly ground black pepper

2 tablespoons (30 ml) extra virgin olive oil

6 cedar planks, purchased

POTATOES

15 small red creamer potatoes, cut in half

2 tablespoons (30 ml) extra virgin olive oil

Salt and freshly ground black pepper

SPICED CITRUS BUTTER

$^1/_4$ cup (60 g) sugar

$^1/_4$ cup (60 ml) water

Juice of 2 oranges

Juice of $^1/_2$ lemon

$^1/_4$ teaspoon (1 g) sambal oelek

$^1/_4$ cup (60 g) unsalted butter

GARNISH

6 limes, halved and grilled

BROILED ALASKAN HALIBUT ON CEDAR PLANKS

WINE PAIRING – ♟ – CHARDONNAY, JORDAN, SONOMA, CALIFORNIA

Preheat oven to 325°F or 165°C.

For salsa, mix all ingredients except herbs in a stainless steel bowl, cover and refrigerate.

For halibut, mix breadcrumbs and herbs into a stainless steel container.

Pat dry halibut steaks, drizzle with lemon juice and season with salt and pepper. Carefully dip each steak into breadcrumb mixture. Arrange halibut steaks on cedar planks, drizzle with olive oil and bake for 15 minutes.

Blanch potatoes in boiling salted water for 8 minutes. Cool in ice water, drain and set aside. In a sauté pan, over medium high heat, warm olive oil and sauté potatoes for 5 minutes or until golden. Season with salt and pepper. Keep warm.

For citrus butter, melt sugar with water in a small saucepan over medium heat and caramelize until golden brown. Remove from heat, add citrus juices and orange ribs and simmer for 10 minutes. Strain through a sieve and transfer into a small saucepan; add sambal oelek and simmer for 5 minutes or until sauce coats the back of a wooden spoon. Remove from heat and whisk in butter a little at a time.

Remove fruit salsa from fridge and mix with fresh herbs.

Serve fish on the plank garnished with grilled lime and sautéed potatoes. Spoon fruit salsa and citrus butter in individual side dishes for all to enjoy as an accompaniment.

Serves 6.

CULINARY NOTES:

Cooking on cedar planks is a great way to infuse a smoky flavor into fish or other items. You are now able to find cedar planks specifically for broiling and/or grilling. Cedar planks can be somewhat expensive and don't last very long. (After all, you are setting them on fire.) You may be able to find bundles of cedar shingles or shims at your local hardware store that will work just as well. Just make sure they are untreated! While grilling, keep a spray bottle filled with water handy and keep an eye on the plank. If it catches fire just spray it out.

6 (6 to 7-ounce) (170 to 200 g) salmon fillets
3 tablespoons (45 ml) extra virgin olive oil

TOMATO COMPOTE
1 pound (450 g) tomatoes
$^1/_4$ cup (60 g) granulated sugar
1 tablespoon (15 ml) water
3 shallots, finely chopped
1 tablespoon (15 g) peeled, chopped fresh ginger
2 cloves garlic, finely chopped
$^1/_4$ cup (60 ml) white wine vinegar

3 tablespoons (45 g) chopped fresh
red chili peppers
$^1/_4$ cup (60 ml) tomato juice
$^1/_4$ cup (60 g) chopped basil
Salt and freshly ground black pepper

ORANGE SAUCE
$^1/_4$ cup (60 ml) freshly squeezed orange juice
Juice of 2 limes
1 tablespoon (15 g) chopped fresh ginger

VEGETABLES
$^1/_4$ cup (60 ml) extra virgin olive oil
2 baby bok choy, cut in half lengthwise
$^1/_2$ pound (250 g) shiitake mushrooms
Salt and freshly ground black pepper

GARNISH
1 carrot, peeled and julienned
2 green onions, julienned
$^1/_4$ cup (60 g) alfalfa sprouts

ORANGE LIME SALMON

WINE PAIRING – – SAUVIGNON BLANC, BRANCOTT, MARLBOROUGH, NEW ZEALAND

Preheat oven to 350°F or 180°C.

Fill a small pan with water and bring it to a boil. Using a sharp knife, gently tear the skin of the tomatoes lengthwise in a couple of spots and place in the boiling water for about 3 minutes. Transfer the tomatoes to a bowl of ice water for 2 minutes or until the skin starts to separate from the tomatoes. Peel, halve, and seed the tomatoes, using a small spoon. Slice the tomatoes into large dice and set aside.

For tomato compote, in a sauté pan over medium heat, melt sugar and water, and caramelize until golden brown. Add the shallots, ginger and garlic, mix well and cook for 2 minutes, then deglaze with the vinegar. Add chili and tomatoes. Season

with salt and black pepper. Quickly bring to a boil and strain tomatoes into a bowl. Return sauce to the burner and stir in tomato juice. Reduce heat and simmer for 10 minutes until sauce has thickened. Adjust seasoning with salt and pepper. Allow sauce to cool, then add diced tomatoes and the basil. Gently mix and serve at room temperature.

For orange sauce, in a small saucepan over medium heat, mix citrus juices and ginger, and simmer for about 15 minutes, until it reaches the consistency of a glaze.

Season salmon with salt and pepper. In a sauté pan over high heat warm olive oil and sear salmon for 1 minute on each side. Arrange on a sheet pan and brush with orange sauce. Cook for 12 to 15 minutes based on desired doneness.

In a sauté pan, over low heat, warm half of olive oil and sauté bok choy for 5 minutes on each side. Season with salt and pepper.

In a separate sauté pan over medium heat, warm the remaining olive oil and sauté the mushrooms for 3 minutes. Season with salt and pepper.

Arrange salmon in the center of warmed plates, top with julienne vegetables, and serve with lukewarm tomato compote.

Serves 6.

CULINARY NOTES:

Bok Choy is sometimes called Chinese cabbage and comes in a variety of sizes. While bok choy is a member of the cruciferous family of vegetables (cabbage, broccoli, Brussels sprouts) it more closely resembles a stalk of celery with deep green leaves and white veins and stalks. It has a mild flavor and is well suited for stir-frying or as a finishing touch in fresh salads.

2 cloves garlic, finely chopped

2 teaspoons (10 g) finely chopped parsley

1/4 cup (60 ml) extra virgin olive oil

Salt and freshly ground black pepper

36 large size shrimp, peeled, deveined,
and tails left on (size 16/20)

1 tablespoon (15 g) unsalted butter

BASIL OIL

1/2 bunch basil, finely chopped

1/4 cup (60 ml) extra virgin olive oil

4 tablespoons (60 g) unsalted butter

VEGETABLES

1/2 pound (250 g) baby star squash, halved

1/2 pound (250 g) baby zucchini, halved

1/2 pound (250 g) asparagus, peeled and trimmed

1/4 pound (120 g) cherry tomatoes, halved

1/4 pound (120 g) baby carrots, halved lengthwise

4 tablespoons (60 ml) extra virgin olive oil

Salt and freshly ground black pepper

1/4 cup (60 ml) fish stock (page 158)

GARNISH

3 lemons, halved

GAMBERONI COTTI IN PADELLA AL PROFUMO DI MARE
Tiger Shrimp with Roasted Garlic and Fresh Herbs

WINE PAIRING – ♸ – PINOT GRIGIO, DANZANTE, VENETO, ITALY

In a non-reactive bowl, mix all ingredients for marinade. Add shrimp, cover and marinate, refrigerated, for 1 hour.

For basil oil, over low heat in a small saucepan, mix olive oil and basil and simmer for 5 minutes.

Coat vegetables with oil and season with salt and black pepper. In a large sauté pan over medium heat sauté vegetables for 10 minutes. Set aside.

In a heavy-bottomed pan over high heat, warm butter and 3 tablespoons (45 ml) of marinade and sauté shrimp for 4 minutes or until they turn pink. Add vegetables and fish stock; adjust seasoning with salt and black pepper and simmer for 5 minutes.

Bring basil oil to a simmer and reduce by half. Remove from heat and whisk in butter a little at a time. Spoon over shrimp and vegetables on each serving plate, and serve immediately.

Serves 6.

MARINADE

1/4 cup (60 ml) extra virgin olive oil
3 cloves garlic, shaved
1 teaspoon (5 g) fresh thyme
2 tablespoons (30 g) julienned basil
2 tablespoons (30 g) chopped parsley

SEAFOOD SKEWER

3 (6 to 7-ounce) (170 to 200 g) lobster tails, cut in half and deveined
12 large size shrimp, peeled, deveined, and tails on (size 16/20)
12 sea scallops (size 10/20)
1 1/2 pounds (700 g) salmon, cubed large
Salt and freshly ground black pepper

6 long skewers (18-inch or 45 cm)

MARINARA SAUCE

1/2 tablespoon (7.5 g) pine nuts
1/2 tablespoon (7.5 ml) extra virgin olive oil
1/2 onion, diced
1 clove garlic, chopped
3 ripe tomatoes, peeled, seeded and diced
1/4 teaspoon (1 g) chopped basil
1/2 tablespoon (7.5 ml) balsamic vinegar
Salt and freshly ground black pepper

SUNDRIED TOMATO BEURRE BLANC

1 teaspoon (5 ml) extra virgin olive oil
2 shallots, minced
1 small onion, diced
6 black peppercorns, crushed
1/4 cup (60 ml) dry white wine
1/2 cup (120 ml) fish stock (page 158)
2 tablespoons (30 ml) white wine vinegar
1/4 cup (60 ml) heavy cream

5 sundried tomatoes, sliced
1 pound (450 g) unsalted butter, room temperature
Salt and freshly ground white pepper

LIGURIAN POTATOES

2 pounds (1 kg) Idaho potatoes, peeled and thickly sliced
1 cup (250 ml) vegetable oil
1 tablespoon (15 ml) garlic oil (purchased)
1 tablespoon (15 ml) onion oil (purchased)
Salt and freshly ground black pepper

1/4 cup (60 g) pine nuts, toasted

VEGETABLES

12 fresh green asparagus, trimmed
12 baby squash
6 baby zucchini, cut diagonally

SPIEDINO DI FRUTTI DI MARE ALLA TOSCANA
Tuscan Seafood Brochette

Preheat oven to 350°F or 180°C.

In a small bowl, mix all ingredients for marinade. Rub into fish and seafood. Thread the fish and seafood through their center on thin skewers. Cover and refrigerate for 1 hour.

For marinara, place pine nuts on a baking sheet in the oven for 2 minutes or until pine nuts are golden brown.

In a small saucepan over medium heat, warm oil and sauté onion for 4 minutes or until translucent. Add garlic and sauté for 1 minute, stirring continually. Do not brown. Add tomatoes and herbs and season with salt and pepper. Cover and simmer for 10 minutes. Add vinegar and 3/4 of the pine nuts, season to taste, stir gently and set aside.

To prepare beurre blanc, in a saucepan over medium heat, warm oil and sauté shallots and onions for 4 minutes. Add crushed peppercorn and deglaze with white wine. Add fish stock and white wine vinegar.

Bring to a simmer and slowly reduce liquid by half. Add cream and sundried tomatoes and simmer for 10 minutes or until sauce coats the back of a wooden spoon. Do not boil. Blend and strain through a fine sieve and whisk in butter a little at a time. Season with salt and pepper. Set aside.

For Ligurian potatoes, blanch potatoes in cold salted water. Bring to a boil and cook for 10 minutes. Cool in cold water, drain and pan-fry in hot oil for 5 to 7 minutes or until potatoes are golden, and crispy to the touch. Transfer on paper towels to absorb excess fat.

In a sauté pan over medium heat, warm garlic and onion oils, add fried potatoes and sauté for 2 minutes. Add toasted pine nuts and enough marinara sauce to coat potatoes. Drizzle with balsamic vinegar and adjust seasoning with salt and pepper. Keep warm.

To grill seafood:

Outdoor grill: Heat to medium/high heat. Place skewers on grill and cook each side for 2 to 4 minutes, turning only once. Season with salt and pepper. Remove from grill and finish in oven for 5 minutes.

Indoor grill: Lightly oil a grill pan. Set temperature to medium/high heat. Place skewers on grill and cook each side for 2 to 4 minutes, turning only once. Season with salt and pepper. Remove from grill and finish in oven for 5 minutes.

Separately blanch asparagus, baby squash and zucchini in boiling salted water for 3 minutes. Keep warm.

Place skewer on warmed plate alongside potatoes and vegetables.

Serve sundried tomato beurre blanc on the side.

Serves 6.

RATATOUILLE

3 tablespoons (45 ml) extra virgin olive oil
1 small (2.5 inches or 6 cm) gingerroot, peeled and crushed
2 cloves garlic, thinly sliced
2 small white onions, diced
2 small eggplants, diced
1 red bell pepper, diced
1 green bell pepper, diced
1 yellow bell pepper, diced
1/3 pound (150 g) shiitake mushrooms, cut in half
2 small zucchini, diced
2 plum tomatoes, diced

1 6-ounce (170 g) can tomato strips
1/8 bunch basil, julienned
1/8 bunch cilantro, chopped
2 tablespoons (30 ml) rice vinegar
Salt and freshly ground black pepper

AIOLI

3 tablespoons (45 ml) rice vinegar
1 egg yolk
1 teaspoon (5 g) Dijon mustard
1 clove garlic, minced
Salt and freshly ground white pepper
1 cup (250 ml) olive oil

1/4 teaspoon (1 g) wasabi powder
1/4 teaspoon (1 ml) soy sauce
1 teaspoon (5 ml) mirin wine

FISH

6 (6 to 7-ounce) (170 to 200 g) tilapia fillets
1/4 cup (60 g) cornmeal
Salt and freshly ground white pepper

GARNISH

3 lemons, halved
Parsley sprigs

CORNMEAL DUSTED TILAPIA

Preheat oven to 350°F or 180°C.

For the ratatouille, in a large sauté pan or wok, over medium heat, warm olive oil and sauté ginger, garlic and onion for 5 minutes. Set aside. Sauté each vegetable type separately for 3 minutes in hot oil. Combine all vegetables into the sauté pan or wok; add fresh and canned tomatoes and season with salt and pepper. Stir well. Add basil, cilantro and rice vinegar and simmer for 20 minutes or until vegetables are cooked. Keep warm.

For aioli, place 3/4 of the rice vinegar, egg yolk, mustard, garlic, salt and pepper in a small glass bowl. While beating mixture, slowly drizzle in oil. Incorporate wasabi, soy sauce, mirin and remaining vinegar.

Stir well. Adjust seasoning, cover and refrigerate until ready to use.

Season tilapia fillets with salt and pepper and dust top side with cornmeal.

Sear fish on both sides, dusted side first, on a hot griddle lightly oiled. Transfer into a baking pan and bake for 5 minutes.

Serve ratatouille and tilapia fillets on warmed plates. Spoon some aioli over fish and garnish with lemon and parsley sprig.

Serve with a side dish of aioli.

Roasted potato wedges would be a great accompaniment to the dish.

Serves 6.

CULINARY NOTES:

Probably the single most important piece of equipment in the kitchen is a good set of sharp knives. Hundreds of sizes and styles are available and there are knives designed for specific tasks. What brand, style or type you use depends on your personal preference and what you are planning to do. Remember, a dull knife is much more dangerous than a sharp one! If you use a dull knife you have to exert more pressure and the blade can twist or slip. Always keep your knives as sharp as possible. Investing in a quality sharpener is a great idea. If you are uneasy about sharpening them yourself have them sharpened professionally.

6 (6-ounce) (170 g) cod fillets

MASHED POTATOES

2 pounds (1 kg) red creamer potatoes,
unpeeled, halved
3/4 cup (175 ml) heavy cream
2 tablespoons (30 g) unsalted butter
Nutmeg
Salt and freshly ground black pepper

CRUST

1/2 pound (250 g) butter, room temperature
2 tablespoons (30 g) margarine
2 tablespoons (30 g) chopped parsley
2 tablespoons (30 g) chopped thyme
3 tablespoons (45 g) chopped chives
3 cloves garlic, finely chopped
2 whole eggs
1 egg yolk
1 cup (250 g) of white bread crumbs
Salt and freshly ground black pepper

SAFFRON SAUCE

1 cup (250 ml) sparkling wine
1 teaspoon (5 g) saffron
1/4 cup (60 ml) heavy cream

GARNISH

6 green onions
3 cherry tomatoes, halved
Rosemary sprigs

ROYAL FILLET OF COD

WINE PAIRING – ♥ – PINOT NOIR, ERATH VINEYARDS, OREGON

Preheat oven to 325°F or 165°C.

To prepare mashed potatoes, place potatoes into salted cold water, bring to a boil and cook until potatoes are easily pierced with the tip of a knife, about 20 minutes. Drain, and press potatoes through a potato ricer into a heated bowl. Stir in cream, butter, and nutmeg. Adjust seasoning with salt and pepper, and keep warm.

For crust, in a large mixing bowl, whip butter and margarine with an electric mixer, at medium to high speed until doubled in size. Add herbs and garlic. Mix well. Add eggs, egg yolk, bread crumbs and adjust seasoning with salt and pepper. Whip for 2 minutes and set aside.

Arrange fillets on a baking pan, pat dry, and season with salt and pepper. Place crust mixture on a sheet of parchment paper; level off to 1/4 inch (1.2 cm) thick. Cut parchment and crust, using a sharp knife, to fit size of each fillet, and gently slide butter on top of each fillet using a warmed spatula. Bake for 15 minutes.

For sauce, in a small saucepan over low heat, infuse sparkling wine with saffron for 5 minutes. Add cream and simmer for 15 minutes or until sauce thickens. Do not boil.

To serve, arrange mashed potatoes in center of each plate, top with fillet and garnish with green onion, tomato and rosemary sprigs.

Serves 6.

CULINARY NOTES:

Why is saffron so expensive?

Scientifically, saffron is the dried stigma of the crocus flower (Crocus sativus). Each blossom produces only 3 stigmas. They must be harvested by hand and it takes over 35,000 flowers to produce one pound of the spice. Fortunately, a small amount is all it takes to season a dish, so it is quite economical.

A simple way to get as much flavor as possible from a few threads of saffron is to place them in the palm of one hand and grind them with the heel of the other. By doing so, you expose a greater amount of surface area and release more of the essence.

HERBED BUTTER

5 tablespoons (75 g) butter
2 tablespoons (30 g) chopped parsley
1 tablespoon (15 g) chopped thyme
1 tablespoon (15 g) chopped chervil

COMBO

4 (6 to 7-ounce) (170 to 200 g) lobster tails
Salt and freshly ground black pepper
$1/4$ cup (60 ml) extra virgin olive oil
2 cloves garlic, minced
12 large size shrimp, peeled, deveined, and tails left on (size 16/20)
Juice of 1 lemon

VEGETABLES

$1/2$ pound (250 g) baby carrots
1 spear broccoli, cut into florets
2 tablespoons (30 g) butter

GARNISH

Dill or tarragon sprigs
2 lemons, halved

LOBSTER AND SHRIMP COMBO

WINE PAIRING – – VOUVRAY, REMY PANNIER, LOIRE, FRANCE

Preheat oven to 450°F or 230°C.

In a small saucepan over medium heat, melt butter and stir in herbs. Keep warm.

With a sharp knife, cut lobster tail shells down the soft underside to expose the flesh. Season with salt and pepper, then brush with some of the butter-herb mixture. Broil lobsters for 6 to 8 minutes until the tail meat is white.

Blanch carrots in boiling salted water for 8 minutes. Cool in ice, drain and set aside.

Blanch broccoli in boiling salted water for 5 minutes. Cool in ice water, drain and set aside.

In a sauté pan over high heat, warm olive oil and sauté garlic and shrimp for 5 to 7 minutes, until shrimp are pink. Season with salt, pepper, and lemon juice.

Reheat carrots and broccoli in hot water at the last minute for a few seconds. In a pan, over medium heat, melt butter and sauté vegetables for 3 to 4 minutes until heated through.

Using a fork, bring lobster meat out of the shell.

Serve on warmed plates surrounded by vegetables and drizzle with warm herbed butter.

Serves 4.

CULINARY NOTES:

Sauté means "to jump" and is a cooking technique where small amounts of food are cooked quickly over high heat. If you need to sauté large quantities of something, it is best to do it in small batches. A large amount of items in a pan, all at once, will drive down the temperature and extend the cooking time. You will also find that a lot of water appears and the items are stewing as opposed to browning.

SAUCE
2 shallots, minced
6 black peppercorns, crushed
1/3 cup (90 ml) dry white wine
Juice of 1 lemon
Juice of 1 lime
1/2 cup (120 ml) heavy cream
1 pound (450 g) unsalted butter, room
temperature
Salt and freshly ground black pepper

SEAFOOD
2 (5 to 6-ounce) (150 to 170 g) lobster tails
4 branches rosemary
2 tablespoons (30 g) Cajun spice
1/4 cup (60 ml) vegetable oil
12 sea scallops
Kosher salt

MARINADE
2 cloves garlic, chopped
1/4 cup (60 ml) extra virgin olive oil
Juice of 1 lemon
Salt and freshly ground black pepper

ASPARAGUS
20 medium asparagus, trimmed and peeled
3 tablespoons (45 ml) extra virgin olive oil
Salt and freshly ground black pepper

GARNISH
2 limes, halved and grilled
Rosemary leaves

Richard Stelmach, Executive Chef, CEC

CAJUN SPICED SCALLOPS AND LOBSTER ROSEMARY SKEWERS WITH LIME BUTTER SAUCE AND GRILLED ASPARAGUS

Chef Richard joined Royal Caribbean as a Chef de Cuisine in September 2002. Born near the Bavarian capital of Munich, Richard began his culinary career at the age of 15. After completing his apprenticeship, Richard worked for some of the world's leading hotel groups, including Sheraton and Hyatt, as well as hotels and restaurants in Germany, the United States and Bermuda. After returning to Germany in 1987, Richard became a Certified Master Chef. He took the opportunity to work in New Zealand for 2 years, then moved to Australia, where he has lived for the past 15 years. In his free time, Richard enjoys riding motorbikes and the occasional skydive.

For sauce, combine shallots, peppercorns, wine, and citrus juices in a saucepan. Simmer for 7 minutes until sauce liquids have reduced by 70 percent. Add cream and simmer for 10 minutes. Do not boil. Remove from heat and whisk in butter a little at a time. Strain through a sieve. Adjust seasoning with salt and pepper.

Preheat grill or a grilling pan at medium high heat.

Cut lobsters in half lengthwise and loosen flesh from the shell.

Prepare marinade by mixing garlic, olive oil, lemon juice, salt and pepper in a small bowl. Brush marinade onto lobster meat and place flesh back into shell. Place meat-side first onto grill and sear for about 2 minutes before turning it over to finish the cooking process for 5 minutes. Keep warm.

Remove all leaves from rosemary branches except for top ones. In a small bowl mix Cajun spice and oil. Pat dry scallops and season with salt. Coat scallops with spice mixture and skewer them onto rosemary branches. Place scallops on grill or grilling pan and cook for 30 seconds on each side. Set aside.

Brush asparagus with olive oil and season with salt and pepper. Place on grill and cook for 3 minutes on each side.

Lay asparagus on warmed plates, top with lobster and scallop skewer. Spoon lemon butter around and garnish with a grilled lime and rosemary leaves.

Serves 4.

MARINADE

2 cloves garlic, crushed
2 teaspoons (10 ml) freshly squeezed lemon juice
1 teaspoon (5 g) ground cumin
1/2 teaspoon (2.5 g) sweet paprika
1/2 teaspoon (2.5 g) powdered saffron
1/2 teaspoon (2.5 g) peeled and ground ginger
2 tablespoons (30 g) chopped cilantro
2 tablespoons (30 g) chopped parsley
2 tablespoons (30 ml) vegetable oil
Salt and freshly ground black pepper

20 jumbo prawns, peeled and deveined
3 tablespoons (45 ml) extra virgin olive oil
Salt and freshly ground black pepper

TOMATO CHARMOULA

2 teaspoons (10 g) cumin seeds
1 teaspoon (5 g) coriander seeds
1 can (16-ounce) (450 g) whole
tomatoes, drained
2 cloves garlic, crushed
2 red chilies, seeded and finely chopped
2 tablespoons (30 g) tomato paste
Juice of 1 lemon
1 teaspoon (5 g) ground sweet paprika

COUSCOUS

1 cup (250 g) couscous
11/2 cups (400 ml) chicken stock, hot
1 yellow bell pepper, finely chopped
1 green bell pepper, finely chopped
2 cloves garlic, crushed
1/2 cup (120 g) chopped green olives
2/3 teaspoon (3 g) ground cumin
3 tablespoons (45 g) chopped parsley

JUMBO PRAWNS WITH MOROCCAN SPICES, TOMATO CHARMOULA AND GREEN OLIVE COUSCOUS

Prepare the marinade in a stainless steel bowl by mixing all ingredients.

Pat dry prawns, and coat with marinade. Cover and refrigerate for 2 hours.

For Tomato Charmoula, place cumin and coriander seeds in a small sauté pan over high heat and dry roast for 15 seconds, until the seeds have released their fragrance. Remove from heat and finely crush. Transfer to a blender with remaining ingredients and blend for about 3 minutes, until a paste consistency is reached. Refrigerate until ready to use.

Place couscous in a bowl and moisten with stock. Cover and set aside for 6 to 8 minutes, until couscous swells. Fluff up with a spoon and cover again for 6 minutes. Fold in peppers, garlic, olives, and cumin, and mix well. Set aside and keep warm. Toss in parsley just before serving.

Heat a heavy skillet over high heat and warm the oil. Sauté prawns for 6 minutes, until they turn pink. Adjust the seasoning with salt and pepper.

On warmed plates, arrange the couscous and top with prawns. Serve with Tomato Charmoula on the side.

Serves 4.

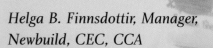

Helga B. Finnsdottir, Manager, Newbuild, CEC, CCA

Chef Helga joined Royal Caribbean International's fleet in August 1999 as the first female Executive Chef to be hired by RCCL. Helga hails from the land of Fire & Ice: Iceland. Her passion for cooking started at the early age of 14, when she worked in leading hotels in Iceland during summer and holiday breaks from school. She studied Provision and Dietary, followed by a 4 year apprenticeship at the Culinary School of Iceland. She has cooked for foreign dignitaries and in fine hotels in Norway and England. Helga began her career at sea in 1993 aboard the QE2. When Helga is not cooking, she enjoys being with family and friends, hiking and biking, and winter sports.

PARSNIPS

5 medium parsnips, peeled and cut
1 1/2 inch (4 cm) thick
6 cloves garlic
2 bay leaves
2 cups (500 ml) milk
2 tablespoons (30 g) butter, room temperature
Salt and freshly ground white pepper

MASHED POTATOES

1 pound (450 g) Idaho potatoes, peeled, quartered
1/3 cup (90 ml) heavy cream
1 tablespoon (15 g) unsalted butter
Salt and freshly ground black pepper

CHORIZO OIL

1/4 cup (60 ml) extra virgin olive oil
1 tablespoon (15 g) ground paprika
Chorizo sausage trimmings
1/4 bunch chives, chopped

SCALLOPS

2 chorizo sausages, sliced 1/2 inch
(1.5 cm) thick at an angle
30 sea scallops
1 tablespoon (15 ml) extra virgin olive oil
Salt and freshly ground white pepper

PETITE SALAD

1/2 cup (120 g) assorted salad leaves such as lollo
rosso, Belgium endive and frisée lettuce
1 plum tomato, seeded and thinly cut lengthwise
Juice of 1 lemon
2 tablespoons (30 ml) extra virgin olive oil
Salt and freshly ground black pepper

SEARED DIVER SCALLOPS AND CHORIZO

WINE PAIRING – GEWURZTRAMINER, DOPFF & IRION, ALSACE, FRANCE

Place parsnips, garlic and bay leaves in milk in a heavy bottom stockpot. Bring to a boil and simmer for 15 minutes or until parsnips are tender and can easily be pierced with the tip of a fork. Strain parsnips, discarding garlic and bay leaves and reserving milk. Transfer into a food processor and blend until smooth. Add butter and enough of reserved milk to form a smooth purée.

For mashed potatoes, place potatoes into salted cold water, bring to a boil and cook until potatoes are easily pierced with the tip of a knife, about 15 minutes. Drain and press potatoes through a potato ricer into a heated bowl. Stir in cream and butter. Incorporate parsnip purée and mix well. Adjust seasoning with salt and pepper. Set aside and keep warm.

For chorizo oil, in a small saucepan over medium heat, warm oil and paprika and sauté chorizo trimmings for 3 minutes. Let cool and strain. Add chives before serving.

In a small frying pan over medium to high heat, warm half of the olive oil and fry chorizo slices on both sides. Remove from the pan and keep warm.

Rinse pan and return to high heat. Pat dry and season scallops with salt and pepper. Warm remaining oil, and sear scallops for 2 minutes on each side, in batches over medium to high heat. Set aside.

To make petite salad, toss salad leaves and tomatoes with lemon juice and olive oil until moist. Season to taste.

To serve, place a spoonful of vegetable purée in the center of warm plates. Arrange scallops and chorizo on top and garnish with the petite salad.

Crown with drops of chorizo oil.

Serves 6.

CULINARY NOTES:

Chorizo sausage is a Spanish sausage made with a mixture of ground pork, pepper and chilies. Chorizo is readily available in most supermarkets but equal substitutions can be made with Andouille, Abruzzo, or Italian Sweet Sausage.

Of the 400 species of scallop available on the open market, sea scallops, bay scallops and calico scallops are the most popular. In the Unites States, bay scallops are favored over sea and calico scallops, as they tend to have a sweeter flavor. Calico scallops have to be steamed open to release the muscle from the shell, thus they arrive to market fully cooked, which makes them less desirable. Sea scallops are much larger and have a more "meaty" quality.

VEGETABLE SALSA

1 yellow bell pepper
4 tablespoons (60 ml) extra virgin olive oil
1 medium red onion, finely diced
2 cloves garlic, chopped
1 zucchini, finely diced
1 fennel, finely diced
1 eggplant, finely diced
2 tomatoes, peeled, seeded and diced
2 tablespoons (30 g) chopped basil
1 tablespoon (15 g) chopped parsley
Salt and freshly ground black pepper

BOUILLABAISSE SAUCE

2 tablespoons (30 ml) extra virgin olive oil
2 leeks, white part only, chopped
1 fennel bulb, chopped
1 clove garlic, chopped
1/2 teaspoon (2 g) saffron
1 tablespoon (15 g) chopped oregano
1/4 teaspoon (1 g) fennel seeds
2 tablespoons (30 ml) Anisette liqueur
4 plum tomatoes, peeled and seeded
1 cup (250 ml) fish stock (page 158)
Salt and freshly ground black pepper

TUNA

2 pounds (1 kg) ahi tuna fillets
2 tablespoons (30 g) tahini paste
3 tablespoons (45 g) black sesame seeds
3 tablespoons (45 g) white sesame seeds
1 tablespoon (15 ml) extra virgin olive oil
1 tablespoon (15 ml) sesame oil
Salt and freshly ground black pepper

GARNISH

1/4 teaspoon (1 g) white sesame seeds
1/4 teaspoon (1 g) black sesame seeds

Thomas Pellocheck, Executive Chef, CEC

Chef Thomas joined Royal Caribbean International in 1998. Born in Frankfurt, Germany, he studied for 3 years in Germany and 2 years in Switzerland. After graduation, Thomas worked in Frankfurt as a Sous Chef for 4 years, then moved to Cairo to work as an Executive Chef for the Sheraton and Intercontinental Hotel chains. During this time, Thomas traveled to Turkey, Russia, Argentina, and then to Munich, Germany, to join the Kempinski Hotel Four Seasons. In his spare time Thomas enjoys reading and gardening.

MEDITERRANEAN TUNA

Preheat oven to 350°F or 180°C.

For salsa, place pepper in an ovenproof dish and drizzle with 2 tablespoons of olive oil. Roast for 20 minutes or until brown and blistery. Remove pepper from oven and place in a small bowl. Cover with plastic wrap. A small, tightly closed paper bag will do also. This loosens the skins and eases peeling. Finely dice the pepper.

In a sauté pan over medium heat warm the remaining oil and sauté the onion and garlic for 5 minutes, until translucent and fragrant. Add vegetables, season with salt and pepper and sauté for 5 minutes. Adjust seasoning, remove from heat and add herbs and pepper. Mix well, cover and refrigerate for 1 hour.

For sauce, in a saucepan over medium heat, warm oil and sauté leeks, fennel and garlic for 3 minutes, until fragrant. Do not brown. Add saffron, oregano and fennel seeds and stir for 30 seconds. Deglaze with the Anisette liqueur. Add tomatoes and stir for 1 minute. Add fish stock and simmer for 20 minutes. Remove from heat and let cool. Adjust seasoning with salt and pepper. Transfer to a blender and blend for 5 minutes, until smooth. Strain through a sieve and set aside. Keep warm.

Coat tuna with tahini paste. Spread sesame seeds on a plate and press tuna firmly onto them on all sides. Heat olive oil and sesame oil in a nonstick skillet over medium high heat. Add tuna, season with salt and pepper and cook until done rare, for 2 minutes on each side or until desired doneness. Remove from heat and cut crosswise into 1/3-inch-thick slices (0.8 cm).

Spoon sauce onto serving plates and fan tuna slices over sauce. Sprinkle with sesame seeds, and serve salsa on the side.

Serves 4.

MUSSELS

1/4 cup (60 g) butter
6 shallots, minced
2 cloves garlic, minced
6 pounds (3 kg) mussels, cleaned and beards
removed (5 to 6 dozen)
3 tablespoons (45 g) flour
2 tablespoons (30 ml) Pernod®
1 cup (235 ml) dry white wine
1/2 teaspoon (2 g) salt
1/4 teaspoon (1 g) freshly ground pepper
2 tablespoons (30 g) chopped parsley

FRIES

Vegetable oil as needed
6 medium potatoes, peeled and cut in
1/4 inch (0.6 cm) strips
2 medium sweet potatoes, peeled and
cut in 1/4 inch (0.6 cm) strips
Salt

GARNISH

Parsley sprigs

MUSSELS MARINIÈRE

In a large saucepan or medium size stockpot, over medium-high heat, melt butter and sauté shallots and garlic for 3 minutes or until transparent, stirring constantly.

Add mussels and flour and mix well. Deglaze with Pernod. Add wine, salt and freshly ground pepper. Cover and simmer 6 to 8 minutes or until shells open, stirring occasionally. Finish with chopped parsley.

In a deep-fat fryer or medium size frying pan, heat about 2 inches (5 cm) of vegetable oil to 400°F or 200°C.

Rinse potato strips in cold water, drain and pat dry with a paper towel.

Gently place an even layer of strips into the hot oil and fry for 7 minutes or until golden brown. Drain on paper towels. Repeat with remaining potatoes. Sprinkle lightly with salt.

Using a ladle, transfer mussels and sauce into heated bowls, discarding any that remained unopened. Garnish each bowl with parsley sprigs.

Serve fries in separate plates.

Serves 8.

Kenneth Johansen, Executive Chef, CEC

Chef Johansen was born in Haslev, Denmark, and began his culinary career with an apprenticeship with SAS/Radisson Hotel, Copenhagen. His first onboard experience was on QE2 in 1996 where he worked as Chef de Partie before joining Royal Caribbean International in 2003 after working for various hotel and restaurants throughout Europe. While on vacation he enjoys traveling, surfing, fine wines and cuisine from around the world.

The main course was prepared to perfection... a true artistry we would not soon forget.

MEAT AND POULTRY

LAMB SHANKS

6 (7-ounce) (200 g) lamb shanks, bone in
$^1/_3$ cup (90 ml) extra virgin olive oil
$^1/_2$ cup (120 g) chopped celery
2 onions, chopped
3 medium carrots, chopped
$^1/_4$ cup (60 g) tomato paste
$^1/_3$ cup (90 ml) red wine
$^1/_4$ cup (60 ml) port wine
3 cups (700 ml) demi-glace (page 159)
1 tablespoon (15 g) chopped thyme
1 tablespoon (15 g) chopped rosemary
1 teaspoon (5 g) whole black peppercorns

1 teaspoon (5 g) juniper berries
2 bay leaves
Salt and freshly ground black pepper

VEGETABLES

$^1/_2$ pound (250 g) carrots, cut into large dice
$^1/_2$ pound (250 g) celery, cut into large dice
$^1/_2$ pound (250 g) celery root, cut into large dice
$^1/_2$ pound (250 g) shallots, halved
$^1/_3$ cup (90 ml) extra virgin olive oil
2 tablespoons (30 g) chopped thyme
2 tablespoons (30 g) chopped rosemary
Salt and freshly ground black pepper

MASHED POTATOES

2 pounds (1 kg) Idaho potatoes, peeled
$^3/_4$ cup (175 ml) heavy cream
2 tablespoons (30 g) unsalted butter
Nutmeg
Salt and freshly ground black pepper

GARNISH

Rosemary and thyme sprigs

BRAISED LAMB SHANKS

WINE PAIRING – ♀ – MALBEC, NAVARRO CORREAS, COLECCION PRIVADA, MAIPU VALLEY, ARGENTINA

Preheat oven to 375°F or 190°C.

Season shanks with salt and pepper. Heat a Dutch oven or heavy stockpot over medium-high heat for 3 to 4 minutes. Add oil and, when it is hot, add lamb shanks in batches. Sear, turning them occasionally until they are well browned on all sides, about 10 minutes. Remove shanks and set aside.

To the same Dutch oven add celery, onion, and carrot. Sauté for 5 minutes or until golden brown. Add tomato paste and mix well. Add wine and port, turn up the heat to medium, and reduce by half.

Add the demi-glace, herbs, and seasonings, and simmer for 10 minutes.

Nestle lamb shanks among vegetables in Dutch oven, making sure that they are covered in liquid. Cover and place in oven. Cook for about 1$^1/_2$ hours, turning occasionally, until meat is falling off the bone. Remove shanks from pot and strain sauce through a cheese cloth. Season to taste with salt and pepper.

Reduce oven heat to 350°F or 180°C.

Place root vegetables in a shallow roasting pan and coat with olive oil, thyme, rosemary, salt and pepper. Roast approximately 45 minutes, until tender.

Place potatoes into salted cold water, bring to a boil and cook until potatoes are easily pierced with the tip of a knife, about 15 minutes. Drain and press potatoes through a potato ricer into a heated bowl. Stir in cream, butter and nutmeg. Adjust seasoning with salt and pepper and keep warm.

Serve each lamb shank in warmed dishes, accompanied by mashed potatoes and roasted vegetables. Spoon sauce over lamb shanks and garnish with fresh herbs.

Serves 6.

CULINARY NOTES:

Braising is a "moist heat" method of cooking tough cuts of meat. Unlike roasting or broiling (dry heat), braising relies on moisture, time and an acid to break down the tough collagen fibers. Acids like tomatoes or wine help tenderize the meat while adding flavor to the finished sauce or gravy. Stewing and pot-roasting are all forms of braising.

Roasting and broiling use a direct heat source and no moisture or acid. The only difference between roasting and baking is that baking does not use an open flame.

6 (7-ounce) (200 g) double-cut pork chops
Salt and freshly ground black pepper
2 tablespoons (30 ml) vegetable oil

RELISH

2 tablespoons (30 g) dark brown sugar
1 small white onion, diced
3 tablespoons (45 ml) port wine
1/4 cup (60 ml) red wine
2 tablespoons (30 ml) red wine vinegar
1/4 cup (60 ml) cranberry juice
2 apples, peeled, cored and diced
1/3 cup (100 g) frozen cranberries

POTATO GRATIN

5 medium potatoes, peeled and thinly sliced
1 1/2 teaspoons (7 g) salt
3 tablespoons (50 g) unsalted butter, melted
1/2 cup (120 ml) half and half
1 cup (250 g) shredded Cheddar cheese

VEGETABLES

1/4 cup (60 g) sweet corn, thawed then grilled
1 tablespoon (15 ml) extra virgin olive oil
2 medium turnips, peeled and cut into
1-inch (2.5 cm) dice
3 carrots, peeled and cut into 1-inch (2.5 cm) dice
1 parsnip, peeled and cut into 1-inch (2.5 cm) dice
1/2 pound (250 g) peeled pumpkin, cut into
1-inch (2.5 cm) dice
3 tablespoons (45 g) unsalted butter
Salt and freshly ground black pepper

GARNISH

1/2 bunch parsley

GRILLED PORK CHOPS

WINE PAIRING – ♟ – SHIRAZ, ROSEMOUNT ESTATE, SOUTH EASTERN AUSTRALIA

Preheat oven to 350°F or 180°C.

Season pork chops with salt and pepper. In a lightly oiled grill pan over high heat, sear each side for approximately 3 minutes. Arrange pork chops on a sheet pan and bake for about 20 minutes, until only minimal juices come out when pricked with a fork.

To prepare relish, caramelize sugar, add onion and stir well for 1 minute. Deglaze with port. Add wine, vinegar and cranberry juice. Bring to a boil, and add apples and cranberries. Simmer about 7 minutes, until the fruit is soft. Remove pan from heat and set aside.

Bring oven temperature to 425°F or 220°C.

For gratin, in a bowl mix potatoes, salt and butter, and toss together. Arrange potato slices in even layers in a 12 inch by 8 inch (30 x 20 cm) baking pan. Pour the cream over potatoes and sprinkle with Cheddar cheese. Cover with foil and bake for 20 minutes. Uncover and bake for another 15 minutes or until potatoes are soft.

Drain and pat dry corn kernels. Using a grilling pan over high heat, warm oil and grill corn for about 3 minutes, until corn turns golden brown in spots. Remove from pan and set aside.

Blanch all the remaining vegetables for 3 minutes and cool in ice water. Drain well.

Melt butter in a sauté pan over medium heat and sauté all the vegetables for 5 minutes or until warmed thorough. Adjust seasoning with salt and black pepper.

On each warmed serving plate, arrange sautéed vegetables and potato gratin, top with a pork chop and relish. Garnish with an herb sprig.

Serves 6.

MARINADE

1 tablespoon (15 ml) black bean sauce
$^{1}/_{3}$ cup (90 ml) hoisin sauce
$^{1}/_{4}$ cup (60 g) honey
3 tablespoons (45 ml) soy sauce
3 tablespoons (45 ml) dry sherry
2 tablespoons (30 ml) sesame oil
1 tablespoon (15 g) sambal oelek
3 cloves garlic, minced
Zest of 1 orange

LAMB

3 racks of lamb with 8 chops each, frenched
2 tablespoons (30 ml) extra virgin olive oil

SWEET POTATO SOUFFLÉS

4 sweet potatoes, skins scrubbed
$^{1}/_{4}$ cup (60 g) sugar
2 tablespoons (30 g) butter
Juice of 1 orange
Zest of $^{1}/_{2}$ orange
2 eggs, separated
Pinch of salt
$^{1}/_{2}$ tablespoon (10 g) butter

BOK CHOY

3 baby bok choy, trimmed and cut lengthwise
1 cup (250 ml) chicken stock (page 158)

GARNISH

1 small purple beet, peeled and sliced very thin
1 cup (250 ml) vegetable oil
Kosher salt

LAMB JUS

2 cloves garlic, crushed
1 vanilla bean, sliced lengthwise
1 tablespoon (15 g) flour
$^{1}/_{2}$ cup (120 ml) red wine
1 cup (250 ml) brown sauce (page 159)

Troy Swindle, Executive Chef, CEC

Troy comes to us from Sydney, Australia. After completing his formal training, he continued within the specialized field of Pastry. Later, he gained practical experience in various hotels and restaurants throughout Australia and acquired several awards including the American Express "Hall of Fame" for the cooking of authentic Australian meats.

He has also worked in various boutique-style resorts around Asia and the Maldives and joined Royal Caribbean International in 2002.

When not working Troy is surfing around the world.

PACIFIC RIM LAMB RACK

Preheat oven to 400°F or 205°C.

To prepare lamb marinade, mix all ingredients in a stainless steel bowl. Coat racks with marinade. Cover and refrigerate for 4 hours.

To make soufflés, place sweet potatoes in salted boiling water and cook until potatoes are easily pierced with the tip of a knife, about 25 minutes. Drain, peel and press potatoes through a potato ricer into a heated bowl. Add all ingredients with the exception of the egg whites and mix well. Set aside.

In a mixing bowl, beat egg whites and pinch of salt with an electric mixer on medium to high speed until they form soft peaks. Fold egg whites into sweet potato mixture.

Evenly pour mixture into 6 buttered soufflé dishes.

Bake for 15 minutes or until firm and lightly browned.

Heat a large skillet over high heat and warm oil. Remove rack from marinade, season with salt and pepper and sear meat

all over for 5 minutes or until nicely browned. Transfer to a roasting pan and bake for 15 to 20 minutes for medium cooked racks. Remove from oven, cover with aluminum foil and let rest for 5 to 10 minutes before carving.

Meanwhile, blanch bok choy in boiling stock for 5 minutes. Drain and keep warm.

In a sauté pan over high heat, warm oil and fry beet slices for 1.5 to 2 minutes or until crisp. Remove from oil and place on paper towels to absorb excess fat. Season with salt.

Place roasting pan over medium heat, add garlic and vanilla and cook until juices caramelize on the bottom and separate from fat. Discard fat. Deglaze with wine and reduce by half. Add flour and cook, stirring constantly for 1 minute. Whisk in brown sauce and simmer for 10 minutes or until sauce coats the back of a wooden spoon. Strain sauce through a fine sieve and keep warm.

Place soufflés in warmed plate. Divide lamb chops among plates. Spoon sauce over lamb and garnish with bok choy and beet chips.

Serves 6.

1 (5 to 6-pound) (2.5 kg) duck

MARINADE
2 cups (500 ml) soy sauce
3 tablespoons (45 g) peeled and chopped ginger
3 sticks lemongrass, outer casing removed, finely chopped
2 kaffir lime leaves, chopped

VEGETABLES
3 tablespoons (45 ml) vegetable oil
1 head Chinese cabbage, cored and sliced thin
2 leeks, julienned
1 red bell pepper, julienned
1 green bell pepper, julienned
Salt and freshly ground black pepper

SAUCE
1 tablespoon (15 g) peeled and chopped ginger
2 cloves garlic, chopped
2 tablespoons (30 ml) sake wine
1 cup (250 ml) brown sauce (page 159)
Salt and freshly ground black pepper

ASIAN DUCK

In a large stainless steel bowl, mix all ingredients for marinade. Pour marinade over duck, cover and refrigerate overnight.

Preheat oven to 375°F or 190°C.

In a large skillet, heat oil over high heat and sear duck. Transfer to an ovenproof dish and roast for 60 minutes, basting every 10 minutes with the pan drippings.

Heat a large sauté pan over medium heat. Warm oil, add cabbage and leeks, and season with salt and pepper. Sauté for 5 minutes, then add peppers. Cook for another 3 minutes. Remove from heat and keep warm.

Remove duck from roasting pan and place on a platter. Place roasting pan over medium heat, add ginger and garlic, stirring continuously for 2 minutes. Deglaze with sake and add brown sauce. Reduce for 10 minutes, simmering. Strain the sauce through a fine sieve, adjust seasoning with salt and pepper, and keep warm.

Quarter the duck and place on warmed plates over cabbage. Drizzle with sauce.

Serves 4.

Thomas Pfennings,
Senior Executive Chef, CEC

Chef Thomas worked for several cruise ship companies before joining the Royal Caribbean family in the role of Senior Executive Chef, overseeing the Radiance class vessels, in January 2004. Thomas was born in the German town of Duren. He first ventured into cooking at the age of 16 in Michelin rated restaurants and went on to complete his Masters after 10 years of cooking professionally. Thomas was lured away from his native land of Germany to experience the world and enhance his culinary abilities. This passion to develop his culinary knowledge and a love for travel have taken him to all corners of the globe cooking for high profile clientele. When not at sea, Thomas' hobbies include dancing and photography.

CHICKEN

1 1/2 pounds (700 g) chicken legs, skinned
and boned
1 1/2 pounds (700 g) chicken breast, skinned,
boned and cut into 2-inch (5 cm) pieces
1/4 cup (60 ml) vegetable oil
2 cloves garlic, chopped
1 tablespoon (15 g) peeled and chopped
fresh ginger
2 tablespoons (30 ml) extra virgin olive oil
Salt and freshly ground black pepper

ORANGE CHILI SAUCE

1/2 cup (120 ml) freshly squeezed orange juice
1/4 cup (60 ml) frozen orange juice
concentrate, thawed
1 cup (250 ml) sweet chili sauce
Zest of 1 orange, minced
Salt

JASMINE RICE

1 1/2 cups (400 g) jasmine rice
1 1/2 cups (400 ml) cold water

1/2 pound (250 g) snow peas
2 tablespoons (30 g) unsalted butter

GARNISH

1 large green bell pepper, julienned
and placed in ice water
1 large red bell pepper, julienned and
placed in ice water
1 large carrot, julienned and placed in ice water
1 large leek, julienned and placed in ice water,
white parts only
1/3 cup (90 g) alfalfa sprouts

ORANGE CHILI CHICKEN

WINE PAIRING – ♟ – JOHANNISBERG RIESLING, CHATEAU ST. MICHELLE, COLUMBIA VALLEY, WASHINGTON

In a large bowl mix chicken with vegetable oil, garlic, ginger, salt and pepper. Cover and refrigerate for at least one hour.

Prepare orange chili sauce by mixing all ingredients in a medium saucepan. Bring mixture to a boil, then reduce heat and simmer for 10 minutes, stirring occasionally. Set aside.

In a large sauté pan over medium-high heat, warm olive oil and sauté chicken pieces for 5 minutes, until browned on all sides. Add orange chili sauce and cook over medium high heat for 10 to 15 minutes until chicken is cooked throughout and nicely glazed.

Rinse rice with cold water 3 to 4 times or until water runs clear. Drain one last time.

Place rice in a pot; add water, let stand for 30 minutes, and bring to a boil. The liquid should be 1 inch (2.5 cm) above the rice. Cook, covered, for 15 minutes. Remove rice from heat, and keep covered on the side of stove for 20 minutes.

Blanch snow peas, drain them and then sauté them in butter for 2 minutes. Season with salt and pepper.

Drain julienned vegetables and mix together with alfalfa sprouts just before serving.

Arrange chicken on a bed of rice and snow peas on a warmed dish, coat with orange-chili sauce and top with julienned vegetables.

Serves 8.

CULINARY NOTES:

There are more than 40,000 different varieties of rice. It is classified according to its size: long-grain, medium-grain and short-grain. Rices are also labeled according to variety: Arborio, Aromatic, Basmati, Glutinous, Jasmine, and Wehani. Each has its own characteristics and imparts its own special flavor and texture to the finished dish. Cooking techniques vary according to the type of rice. Some require soaking overnight while others need to be sautéed before boiling.

CHIMICHURRI SAUCE

Juice of 1 lemon
1/3 cup (90 g) minced fresh parsley
1 clove garlic, minced
2 shallots, small diced
2 tablespoons (30 g) minced fresh basil
2 tablespoons (30 g) minced fresh mint
1 teaspoon (5 g) minced hot pepper
1/2 tablespoon (7.5 ml) Worcestershire sauce
1 tablespoon (15 ml) soy sauce
1/4 red bell pepper, small diced
1/4 green bell pepper, small diced
1/2 cup (120 ml) extra virgin olive oil
Salt and freshly ground black pepper

GARLIC CONFIT

1 head of garlic, peeled and shaved
1/3 cup (90 ml) extra virgin olive oil

BALSAMIC VINAIGRETTE

1/4 cup (60 ml) balsamic vinegar
1/2 cup (120 ml) extra virgin olive oil
Salt and freshly ground black pepper

PORTABELLA

3 large portabella mushrooms, stalks and gills removed
2 tablespoons (30 ml) extra virgin olive oil
1/4 bunch parsley, finely chopped
1/4 bunch basil, finely chopped
Salt and freshly ground black pepper

SAUTEED SPINACH

1 tablespoon (15 ml) extra virgin olive oil
1/2 onion, finely chopped
1/2 pound fresh spinach, stems off
Salt and freshly ground black pepper

STEAKS

6 (5-ounce) (150 g) New York strip steaks
Salt and freshly ground black pepper

FOCACCIA

6 individual rosemary focaccia, grilled (purchased)

GARNISH

1 cup (250 g) mesclun mix

OPEN FACE STEAK SANDWICH

WINE PAIRING – – WHITE ZINFANDEL, BERINGER, CALIFORNIA

Preheat oven to 325°F or 165°C.

For chimichurri sauce, combine all ingredients in a stainless steel bowl and slowly whisk in oil. Cover and refrigerate for 24 hours.

In a small saucepan over low heat, simmer garlic in olive oil for 20 minutes or until garlic reaches a light golden color.

To make vinaigrette, place vinegar in a small non-reactive bowl and slowly whisk in olive oil. Season with salt and black pepper to taste.

Cut portabella mushrooms into 5 slices at an angle. Brush with garlic confit and season with salt and pepper.

To Grill Mushrooms:

Outdoor grill: Heat to medium high. Place mushroom slices on the grill. Cook each slice for 2 to 3 minutes, turning only once. Remove from the grill and set on a tray.

Indoor grill: Lightly oil a grill pan. Set temperature to medium/high heat. Place mushroom slices on the grill. Cook each slice for 2 to 3 minutes, turning only once. Remove and set on a tray.

Top grilled mushroom slices with garlic confit and chopped herbs. Keep warm in the oven.

For spinach, in a saucepan over medium heat, warm oil and sauté onions for 4 minutes or until translucent. Add spinach and seasoning and sauté for 2 minutes. Drain excess water.

For steaks, preheat broiler for 5 minutes over high heat. Broil steaks to the desired degree of doneness, about 5 minutes for rare and 7 minutes for medium. Season with salt and pepper. Transfer to a warmed platter, tent loosely with aluminum foil and let stand for 10 minutes. Cut each steak in half at an angle.

Place focaccia on warmed plates, top with spinach, mushrooms, steaks and 2 spoonfuls of chimichurri sauce. Garnish with mesclun mix and drizzle with balsamic vinaigrette.

Serves 6.

IRISH CABBAGE

2 small Savoy cabbage, finely shredded
2 carrots, peeled and finely sliced

1 tablespoon (15 ml) extra virgin olive oil
1 tablespoon (15 g) butter
8 slices of bacon, diced
4 shallots, finely sliced
1/4 cup (60 ml) chicken stock (page 158)
Salt and freshly ground black pepper

LAMB

6 (7-ounce) (200 g) lamb tenderloin
2 tablespoons (30 ml) extra virgin olive oil
2 tablespoons (30 ml) sherry vinegar
1/2 bottle Cabernet wine
1 cup (250 ml) chicken stock (page 158)
Salt and freshly ground black pepper

MASHED POTATOES

2 pounds (1 kg) Idaho potatoes,
peeled, quartered
3/4 cup (175 ml) heavy cream
2 tablespoons (30 g) unsalted butter
Nutmeg
Salt and freshly ground black pepper

GARNISH

1/4 bunch parsley, finely chopped

IRISH LAMB AND CABBAGE

Andrew Cartwright, Executive Chef, CEC

Born in Bradford, England, Chef Andrew joined Royal Caribbean International in 2004. He is a graduate from the Thomas Danby Culinary School in Leeds, England and is a Certified Executive Chef from the American Culinary Federation.

He trained in the best restaurants in Europe before finally giving in to his second passion and deciding to travel the world on board first class vessels as Executive Chef thus combining his love of food and travel.

When not cooking he enjoys playing golf, racing his Yamaha One motorcycle and spending time with his family and friends. Andrew also enjoys working in small restaurants around his hometown to keep up with current food trends.

Blanch cabbage in boiling salted water for 2 minutes. Remove from boiling water, cool in ice, drain and set aside. Return salted water to a boil, blanch carrots for 2 minutes. Cool in ice, drain and set aside.

In a pan, over medium heat, warm oil and butter and sauté bacon and shallots for 3 minutes. Add cabbage, carrots and stock and cook for 10 minutes or until vegetables are cooked through. Season with salt and pepper.

Season lamb with salt and pepper. In a sauté pan over high heat, warm oil and sear lamb on both sides. Reduce heat to medium and cook for 6 to 8 minutes, turning occasionally. Remove lamb and set aside. Deglaze sauté pan with sherry vinegar, add wine and reduce by half.

Add chicken stock and reduce until sauce is thick enough to coat the back of a spoon. Pass through a fine sieve or cheesecloth. Adjust seasoning with salt and pepper.

Place lamb back in sauce, cover and set aside.

Just before serving, slice loins diagonally into 4 slices each.

For mashed potatoes, place potatoes into cold, salted water, bring to a boil and cook until potatoes are easily pierced with the tip of a knife, about 15 minutes. Drain and press potatoes through a potato ricer into a heated bowl. Stir in cream, butter and nutmeg. Adjust seasoning with salt and pepper.

Place vegetables in the center of warm plates. Top with lamb. Ladle with sauce.

Serve mashed potatoes garnished with chopped parsley in a side dish.

Serves 6.

MARINADE

1/2 cup (120 ml) extra virgin olive oil
2 cloves garlic
1/4 cup (60 g) chopped basil
1 tablespoon (15 g) chopped rosemary
8 juniper berries
2 tablespoons (30 g) Dijon mustard
1 tablespoon (15 g) paprika

4 duck breasts, boned, shaved of
excess of fat and skin scored with
a diamond pattern

POTATO CAKES

2 pounds (1 kg) Idaho potatoes
1/4 cup (60 g) unsalted butter, room temperature
Salt and freshly ground pepper

SAUCE

1 1/2 cups (400 g) fresh blueberries
1 tablespoon (15 g) coarse black pepper
1/4 cup (60 g) sugar
1 cup (250 ml) port wine
1 cup (250 ml) red wine
1 tablespoon (15 g) unsalted butter

GARNISH

Sage leaves, deep fried

CRACKED BLACK PEPPER-BLUEBERRY DUCK BREAST AND POTATO CAKES

For the marinade, combine all ingredients and blend until smooth. Rub marinade into duck breasts. Cover and refrigerate for 1 hour.

Preheat oven to 425°F or 220°C.

Scrub and dry potatoes. Place on a sheet pan, season with salt and pierce skin in a few places with a fork. Bake for 1 hour or until tender.

While hot, halve potatoes and scoop out flesh. Mash potatoes, add half of butter, salt and pepper and shape into individual cakes.

Sauté potato cakes in remaining butter in a small sauté pan over medium heat until golden on both sides.

Remove breasts from marinade. Sear duck, skin side down in a sauté pan over high heat until golden brown and slightly crisp. Allow the fat to render and discard the excess. Lower heat to medium, turn breasts and continue to cook for an additional

6 minutes, until meat is cooked to the doneness required, slightly firm to the touch and nicely golden. Let rest for 5 minutes, loosely covered with aluminum foil.

For sauce, in a small saucepan over medium-high heat, combine 3/4 cup (175 g) of the blueberries, pepper, sugar, port and wine, bring to a boil and simmer for about 20 minutes or until berries are falling apart. Pour mixture through sieve into a small saucepan, pressing on berries to extract all the juice. Over medium heat simmer sauce and remaining blueberries for 5 minutes. Remove from heat and slowly whisk in the butter. Keep warm.

Using a sharp knife cut the duck breasts on the bias into 1/2-inch (1.2 cm) slices.

Place potato cakes in the center of warmed plates; arrange duck slices in a fan on top. Spoon the sauce around and garnish with deep fried sage.

Serves 4.

Allan Daly, Executive Chef, CEC

Chef Allan joined Royal Caribbean International in March 1992. Allan was born in Ontario, Canada. After graduating from high school, Allan set out to explore and work in the great West of Canada, then returned to Ontario to attend the prestigious George Brown School of Culinary Arts in Toronto. He earned his Chef's degree in 3 years, graduating with honors. Allan went on to work in Rieden, Switzerland, before returning to North America. Allan worked for many 4- and 5-star resort establishments before embarking on his life at sea. Allan resides in Victoria, British Columbia with his wife Birgitta and son Markus. He enjoys spending his vacation time exploring the wonders of Western Canada.

VEAL SCALOPPINE

12 veal scaloppine, 1 1/2 to 2 inches (5 cm) thick
12 sage leaves
12 prosciutto slices, thin
Salt and freshly ground black pepper
1/2 cup (120 g) flour
6 tablespoons (85 ml) clarified unsalted butter
1/4 cup (60 ml) Marsala
1 cup (250 ml) dry white wine
2 cups (500 ml) veal demi-glace (page 159)
1 tablespoon (15 g) unsalted butter

RISOTTO

1/3 cup (90 g) dried porcini mushrooms
7-8 cups (1.5 to 2 L) chicken or vegetable
stock (page 158)
1/4 cup (60 ml) extra virgin olive oil
2 shallots, finely chopped
1 clove garlic, chopped
3 cups (750 g) Arborio rice
1/2 cup (120 ml) dry white wine
2 tablespoons (30 g) unsalted butter
1/4 cup (60 g) Parmesan cheese, freshly grated
Salt and freshly ground white pepper

1 tablespoon (15 ml) extra virgin olive oil
1/3 cup (100 g) fresh crimini mushrooms,
thickly sliced

12 baby zucchini, halved lengthways
1 tablespoon (15 ml) extra virgin olive oil
Salt and freshly ground black pepper

GARNISH
Fresh sage leaves

SALTIMBOCCA ALLA ROMANA
Veal Saltimbocca Romana

WINE PAIRING – 🍷 – CHIANTI CLASSICO RISERVA, CASTELLO DE GABBIANO, TUSCANY, ITALY

Flatten the veal fairly thin with the flat side of a mallet. Season with salt and black pepper, then place a fresh sage leaf and prosciutto on top of each scaloppine. To keep the prosciutto in place during cooking, place the ready meat between layers of plastic wrap and pound gently with the flat side of the mallet.

Dredge meat in flour. Shake off any excess.

Heat clarified unsalted butter in a large skillet and sauté veal for 1 minute on each side, starting with ham side down. Remove from pan and keep warm.

Using the same pan, add Marsala, then the wine and reduce slightly. Add veal demi-glace and reduce by half. Remove from heat. Strain into a small saucepan and whisk in butter. Keep warm.

For risotto, place dried mushrooms in warm water for 15 minutes.

In a saucepan over medium heat, bring stock to a simmer and maintain over low heat.

In a large saucepan, heat olive oil over medium heat. Add shallots and garlic and sauté until translucent, about 4 minutes Add dried mushrooms and rice and stir until each grain is well coated with oil, about 3 minutes. Add wine and stir until it is completely absorbed. Add stock to rice a ladleful at a time, stirring frequently after each addition until absorbed. Make sure the rice never gets dry. Season with salt and white pepper.

When rice is tender, about 20 minutes, add butter and grated cheese. Set aside.

Over medium heat, in a small saucepan, warm olive oil and sauté crimini mushrooms for 3 minutes.

Over low heat add a little of remaining stock to rice and sautéed mushrooms, and warm up, about 1 minute.

Season zucchini and rub with olive oil. Heat a grilling pan over medium heat and grill for five minutes, turning once.

Serve risotto on a warmed plate, topped with veal. Garnish with grilled zucchini and a spoonful of Marsala reduction.

Serves 6.

CULINARY NOTES:

Butter is clarified to eliminate milk solids. To clarify, place butter in a small container and slowly heat until the proteins in the unsalted butter coagulate and rise to the surface while the solids sink to the bottom. Skim off the coagulated proteins from the top and carefully ladle out the now clarified butter, leaving the milk solids at the bottom.

VEAL CHOPS

Juice of 2 lemons
1/4 cup (60 ml) extra virgin olive oil
Salt and freshly ground black pepper
6 (7-ounce or 200 g) veal chops

GALETTES

1/2 teaspoon (2 ml) vegetable oil
2 ounces (60 g) bacon, diced
1/2 onion, finely chopped
1 clove garlic, crushed
1/3 cup (100 g) cream cheese

1 tablespoon (15 ml) vegetable oil

4 large russet potatoes, peeled and grated
(do not rinse)
3 tablespoons (45 g) clarified butter
Salt and freshly ground white pepper

MERLOT GLAZE

1 tablespoon (15 ml) vegetable oil
1 large carrot, finely chopped
2 onions, finely chopped
1 leek, cleaned and finely chopped
1/4 cup (60 g) finely chopped celery
1/2 cup (120 ml) Merlot wine
2 cups (450 ml) chicken stock (page 158)
2 tablespoons (30 g) butter
Salt and freshly ground black pepper

VEGETABLES

3 large carrots, cut in ribbons using a
vegetable peeler
3 zucchinis, cut in ribbons using
a vegetable peeler
1 tablespoon (15 g) butter
Salt and freshly ground white pepper

GARNISH

6 basil leaves, fried

GRILLED VEAL CHOPS
On Crispy Potato Galette with Merlot Glaze

Patrick McCabe, Executive Chef, CEC

Chef Patrick started his culinary career in his mother's kitchen, learning the basics from this accomplished cook.

He completed his apprenticeship at Sheeky's Restaurant, a renowned seafood restaurant in London's Theater district. There he refined his skills by participating in an exchange program with the Badrutt's Palace Hotel of St Moritz.

Patrick joined Royal Caribbean International in 2002 after working for numerous deluxe hotels in Europe such as the Park Lane Hotel in Piccadilly. From there he emigrated to Australia, experimenting the with "bush tucker" cuisine while working at the Victorian Art Center and the Grand Chancellor Hotel in Melbourne.

When not on board he enjoys bicycling and spending time with his family.

Preheat oven to 350°F or 180°C.

For veal chops, in a stainless steel bowl, mix lemon juice, olive oil, salt and pepper. Coat veal chops with marinade. Cover and refrigerate for 1 hour.

For galettes, in a sauté pan over medium heat, warm oil and sauté bacon for 2 minutes or until crispy; add onion and garlic and cook for 3 minutes or until translucent; add cream cheese and mix well. Set aside.

In a large stainless steel bowl, mix potatoes with butter and seasoning.

Divide 1/2 of potato mixture into 6 lightly oiled small molds and press firmly. Fill in with cream cheese mixture and top with remaining potatoes. Press firmly and bake for 35 minutes.

For glaze, in a saucepan over medium heat, warm oil and sauté vegetables for 3 minutes. Deglaze with wine and reduce by half. Add chicken stock, bring to a boil and simmer for 30 minutes, skimming regularly or

until sauce coats the back of a wooden spoon. Remove from heat, strain into a small saucepan, rectify seasoning with salt and pepper and whisk in butter a little at a time. Keep warm.

Heat a grilling pan over high heat. Sear each side of chops for approximately 3 minutes. Arrange chops on a sheet pan and bake for about 20 minutes for medium cooked chops.

Blanch carrots in boiling salted water for 2 minutes. Drain and set aside.

Blanch zucchini in boiling salted water for 2 minutes. Drain and set aside.

In a small sauté pan over medium heat, melt butter and sauté vegetables for 2 minutes. Season with salt and pepper. Keep warm.

Arrange galette in the center of a warmed plate. Top with veal chop and garnish with vegetable ribbons and a spoonful of Merlot reduction. Finish with fried basil leaves.

Serves 6.

STEW

4 pounds (2 kg) deer (venison),
cut in 1 1/2 inch (3.6 cm) cubes

1/2 cup (120 g) celery, cut in
1 1/2 inch (3.6 cm) cubes

3 medium carrots, cut in 1 1/2 inch
(3.6 cm) cubes

1 red onion, cut in half

4 cloves garlic, finely chopped

2 bay leaves

12 juniper berries

4 stems fresh thyme

1 stem rosemary

2 bottles Merlot

1/2 cup (120 ml) apple cider vinegar

3 tablespoons (45 ml) vegetable oil

Salt and freshly ground black pepper

ROUX

1/4 cup (60 g) butter
1/4 cup (60 g) flour

POLENTA

2 quarts (1.8 L) boiling water
2 tablespoons (30 ml) extra virgin olive oil
2 cups (500 g) cornmeal
Salt and freshly ground black pepper

GARNISH

Rosemary sprigs

URNER GÄMSCHPFÄFFER BRAISED DEER (VENISON) URI STYLE

For stew, place deer meat, vegetables, herbs, wine and vinegar in a glass or stainless steel bowl. Cover and refrigerate for 3 to 5 days.

Separate meat, vegetables and marinade.

In a stockpot over high heat, bring marinade to a boil. Remove foam with a skimmer.

In a large stockpot, over high heat, warm oil and sauté deer meat, turning occasionally for 15 minutes or until meat is golden. Add vegetables, herbs, and marinade until meat is completely covered. Adjust seasoning with salt and pepper. Bring to a boil and simmer for 1 1/2 hours or until meat is tender.

For roux, in a sauté pan over medium heat, melt butter, stir in flour and roast until golden brown, stirring constantly.

Strain deer meat and vegetables, whisk in roux a little at a time until sauce thickens and coats the back of the spoon. Place meat and vegetables in sauce, rectify seasoning with salt and pepper, cover and keep warm.

To prepare polenta, in boiling, salted water, add olive oil and slowly stir in polenta over low heat, whisking constantly. Cook for 10 minutes or until polenta is soft. Season with salt and pepper.

Arrange polenta in the center of warmed plate, spoon stew around and garnish with rosemary sprigs.

Serves 6.

Marco Reist, Executive Chef, CEC

Born in Bern, Switzerland, Executive Chef Marco Reist brings with him years of experience from leading hotels around the world.

After a three years professional apprenticeship in a 5 star hotel near the Swiss Alps, he worked for various deluxe hotels throughout Europe. He gained his international experience by being part of a select start up team specializing in the openings of hotels in both Mexico and South America.

He joined his first cruise ship in 2000 and became part of Royal Caribbean International in 2003.

When not on board, Marco enjoys cooking for his family, tending his herb garden and traveling around the world.

BEEF

2 to 2¹/₂ pounds (1 to 1.5 kg) beef
tenderloin, trimmed and tied
Salt and freshly ground black pepper
2 tablespoons (30 ml) vegetable oil

1 pound (450 g) crimini mushrooms, whole
3 tablespoons (45 ml) extra virgin olive oil

MASHED POTATOES

2 pounds (1 kg) Idaho potatoes,
peeled, quartered
³/₄ cup (175 ml) heavy cream
2 tablespoons (30 g) unsalted butter
Nutmeg
Salt and freshly ground black pepper

18 fresh green asparagus, trimmed

GREEN PEPPERCORN SAUCE

2 shallots, finely chopped
2 tablespoons (30 g) unsalted butter
¹/₂ cup (120 g) green peppercorns, canned
and drained
2 tablespoons (30 ml) brandy
¹/₂ cup (120 ml) demi-glace (page 159)
¹/₃ cup (90 ml) heavy cream
Salt and freshly ground black pepper

GARNISH

Rosemary sprigs

WHOLE ROASTED BEEF TENDERLOIN

WINE PAIRING – 🍷 – CABERNET SAUVIGNON RESERVE, ROBERT MONDAVI, NAPA, CALIFORNIA

Preheat oven to 350°F or 180°C.

Season beef with salt and black pepper. In a heavy sauté pan over medium high heat, warm oil and sear beef on all sides. Place beef on a rack in a broiling pan. Roast for 30 minutes for rare or until the desired doneness, turning once. Remove from oven and let rest.

For mashed potatoes, place potatoes into salted cold water, bring to a boil and cook until potatoes are easily pierced with the tip of a knife, about 15 minutes. Drain and press potatoes through a potato ricer into a heated bowl. Stir in cream, butter and nutmeg. Adjust seasoning with salt and pepper and keep warm.

Blanch asparagus in boiling, salted water for 3 minutes. Cool in ice water, drain, and set aside. Reheat in hot water, at the last minute, for a few seconds.

In a small saucepan over high heat, warm olive oil and sauté mushrooms for 5 minutes or until nicely browned. Keep warm.

For sauce, sauté shallots in butter over medium heat until translucent. Add peppercorns and then brandy. Stir well. Add demi-glace and let simmer for about 15 minutes. Add cream and adjust consistency by simmering for a few minutes to reduce if too thin. Season with salt and black pepper.

Slice tenderloin and arrange on warmed plates over mashed potatoes and three asparagus per plate. Finish with green peppercorn sauce. Garnish with mushrooms and rosemary sprig.

Serves 6.

CULINARY NOTES:

When roasting or broiling meats it is best to let it "rest" for 10 to 20 minutes before slicing. As the meat cooks, the internal juices are drawn toward the surface. If you slice the meat right after it comes out of the oven, the juices will drain out and your lovely and well dressed roast will be dry and lifeless.

Remove the roast from the oven about 10 degrees short of the desired doneness and allow it to rest, covered, for 10 to 20 minutes. The meat will continue to cook or "carry over" and standing time will assist in achieving the perfect finished cooking temperature.

WASABI SAUCE

2 to 3 teaspoons (10 g) wasabi powder
1 cup (250 ml) Chardonnay wine
1 cup (250 ml) heavy cream
Juice of 1/2 lemon
1/2 teaspoon (2 g) salt
2 tablespoons (30 g) unsalted butter,
   room temperature

FILETS

4 (6 to 7-ounce) (170 to 200 g) filet
   mignon steaks
2 tablespoons (30 ml) extra virgin olive oil
Salt and freshly ground black pepper

RICE BALLS

2 cups (500 g) sushi rice
2 cups (500 ml) cold water
1/2 teaspoon (2 g) Mirin wine
1/2 teaspoon (2 g) sake
1 teaspoon (5 g) icing sugar

1 cup (250 ml) cold water
1/4 cup (60 g) corn starch
3 egg yolks
1/4 cup (60 g) all purpose flour
Salt
1 cup (250 ml) vegetable oil for frying

STIR-FRIED VEGETABLES

1 1/2 tablespoons (25 ml) vegetable oil
1/2 tablespoon (10 ml) sesame oil
2 green onions cut lengthwise
1 clove garlic, crushed
1/4 fresh red chili, seeded and sliced
1/2 cup (120 g) snow peas, blanched
1/2 cup (120 g) cauliflower florettes, blanched
1/2 cup (120 g) broccoli florettes, blanched
1/4 cup (60 g) carrots, cut diagonally and
   blanched
1/2 red bell pepper, cut in strips
2 tablespoons (30 ml) soy sauce
1 tablespoon (15 ml) fish sauce
1 tablespoon (15 ml) oyster sauce
3 tablespoons (45 ml) vegetable stock (page 158)

*Wim Van Der Pas, Culinary Trainer
for the Royal Culinary Academy at Sea*

Chef Wim joined Royal Caribbean International in 2003. Wim was born in Vught, Netherlands, but has lived in New Zealand for the past 17 years with his wife, Christine, and their three children Cameron, Zeranya and Rinaldo. His culinary career began at the age of 12, working after school in restaurants as a pot washer. After attending culinary school in the Netherlands, he worked throughout Europe and New Zealand in some of those country's most renowned establishments. When not on board, Wim enjoys playing soccer with his children or watching a good rugby game.

FILET MIGNON GOES EAST

Prepare wasabi by mixing the powder with 2 to 3 teaspoons (10 to 15 ml) of water until it reaches a paste consistency.

To make sauce, bring wine to a boil in a medium size saucepan and simmer for about 10 minutes until wine has reduced by half. Stir in cream and simmer for 5 minutes, until mixture is thick enough to coat the back of a spoon. Add lemon juice, salt and wasabi paste. Remove from heat and whisk in butter a little at a time. Adjust seasoning with salt if necessary. Keep warm.

Rinse rice with cold water 3 to 4 times or until water runs clear. Drain one last time.

Place rice in a pot; add water, let stand for 30 minutes, and bring to a boil. The liquid should be 1 inch (2.5 cm) above the rice. Cook, covered, for 15 minutes. Remove rice from heat, and keep covered on the side of stove for 20 minutes. In a small saucepan combine wine, sake, and icing sugar. Heat mixture until sugar is dissolved. Place rice into a sushi barrel or large bowl, pour vinegar mixture evenly over rice, mix and let cool.

To make batter, sift flour and corn starch into a large bowl, whisk in egg yolks and water. Season with salt and mix well.

Once rice has cooled, form it into 2-inch (5 cm) balls. Dip balls in the batter and fry until golden brown.

For the stir fry, heat wok or frying pan over medium heat, warm oils, and add green onion, garlic and chili. Stir fry for 1 minute; add vegetables and stir fry for 2 minutes over high heat. Stir in sauces and stock. Cook for 5 minutes, until the vegetables are tender but still with a little crunch.

Rub steaks with the oil, and season with salt and pepper.

Heat grill and sear filets on both sides. Reduce heat and cook until desired doneness.

Arrange stir-fried vegetables in the center of warmed plates. Place meat on top. Garnish with tempura rice balls. Spoon some wasabi sauce over meat and serve immediately.

Serves 4.

MARINADE

3 cloves garlic, peeled and shaved
1 tablespoon (15 g) thyme
1/4 cup (60 ml) extra virgin olive oil
1/4 cup (60 ml) white wine
Salt and freshly ground black pepper
4 (5-ounce) (150 g) veal tenderloin medallions
1/4 cup (60 g) all-purpose flour
1 tablespoon (15 ml) vegetable oil
2 (6-ounce) (170 g) lobster tails

MASHED POTATOES

2 pounds (1 kg) Idaho potatoes
4 ounces (120 g) mascarpone cheese
1/4 cup (60 ml) milk
Salt and freshly ground white pepper

BEURRE BLANC

2 shallots, minced
6 black peppercorns, crushed
1/3 cup (90 ml) dry white wine
Juice of 1 lemon
3 tablespoons (45 ml) cider vinegar
1/2 cup (120 ml) heavy cream
1 pound (450 g) unsalted butter, room temperature
1/2 bunch basil, finely chopped
Salt and freshly ground black pepper

BROWN SAUCE

2 shallots, minced
1/4 cup (60 ml) brandy
3/4 cup (175 ml) brown sauce (page 159)

GARNISH

12 asparagus spears, trimmed and peeled

ROYAL VEAL, BASIL BEURRE BLANC, AND MASCARPONE MASHED POTATOES

In a stainless steel bowl, mix all ingredients for marinade. Remove lobster meat from shells. Place two skewers in lobster meat to keep them straight. Marinate tails for 2 hours, covered and refrigerated.

Place potatoes into salted cold water, bring to a boil and cook until potatoes are easily pierced with the tip of a knife, about 15 minutes. Drain and press potatoes through a potato ricer into a heated bowl. Add mascarpone cheese and milk. Adjust seasoning and keep warm.

For the beurre blanc, combine shallots, peppercorns, wine, lemon juice, and vinegar in a saucepan. Simmer for 7 minutes until the sauce liquids are reduced by two-thirds. Add cream and simmer for 10 minutes. Do not boil. Remove from heat and whisk in the butter a little at a time. Strain through a sieve. Adjust seasoning with salt and pepper, stir in basil and keep warm.

Preheat oven to 400°F or 200°C.

Pat dry veal medallions, season with salt and pepper, and dredge in flour. Shake off any excess. In a sauté pan over high heat, warm oil and pan-sear both sides for 5 minutes or until golden brown. Transfer medallions to a baking sheet. For brown sauce, pour off any excess oil from the saucepan, add shallots and sauté for 3 minutes, until translucent, and deglaze with brandy. Add brown sauce and simmer until sauce has reduced by half. Strain and keep warm.

In a sauté pan over medium-high heat, sear lobster tails for 5 minutes on each side. Remove from heat, remove skewers and cut into 1 inch (2.5 cm) thick medallions.

Blanch asparagus in boiling, salted water for 3 minutes.

To serve, transfer potatoes to a piping bag and pipe into the center of warm plates, top with veal, then lobster medallions. Spoon some beurre blanc over the lobsters and some brown sauce around the plate. Garnish with asparagus.

Marco Marrama,
Senior Executive Chef, CEC

Chef Marco joined Royal Caribbean International in 2003 as an Executive Sous Chef on board Voyager of the Seas. Marco was born and raised in Rome, Italy. He attended Culinary school in Rome and obtained a diploma in classic French Cuisine, as well as a culinary diploma from the Cordon Bleu school in Rome. He has worked in fine dining restaurants in Europe, Australia, and at the Royal Palace in Skirat, Morocco. When not cooking, Marco enjoys painting, playing tennis and taking care of his bonsai.

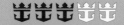

Serves 4.

A rhapsody of fresh, colorful ingredients made our vegetarian main course memorable.

VEGETARIAN

TOFU

3 packages firm tofu, sliced lengthwise

Salt and freshly ground black pepper

$1/3$ cup (90 ml) vegetable oil

STIR-FRIED VEGETABLES

$1/3$ cup (90 ml) sesame oil

3 cloves garlic, minced

$1/2$ pound (250 g) onions, cut into thick julienne

$1/2$ pound (250 g) red bell peppers, cut into thick julienne

8 shiitake mushrooms, trimmed and halved

$1/2$ pound (250 g) bok choy, cut into $1/2$-inch (1.2 cm) slices

4 ounces (120 g) spinach, trimmed

Salt and freshly ground black pepper

RED CURRY SAUCE

1 tablespoon (15 ml) vegetable oil

1 red onion, chopped

3 cloves garlic, minced

1 tablespoon (15 g) peeled and chopped fresh ginger

1 medium tomato, peeled, seeded and chopped

2 teaspoons (10 g) ground cumin

1 teaspoon (5 g) masala, purchased in any Indian food store

2 tablespoons (30 g) red curry paste

$1/2$ cup (120 ml) coconut milk

2 tablespoons (30 g) chopped cilantro

Salt and freshly ground black pepper

GARNISH

Chives

ASIAN FRIED TOFU

WINE PAIRING – ❦ – RIESLING, YALUMBA Y SERIES, SOUTH AUSTRALIA

Lightly season tofu with salt and freshly ground black pepper. Heat vegetable oil in a large skillet over medium heat and sauté tofu until it is golden brown.

For stir-fry, in a wok or large sauté pan, heat sesame oil and sauté minced garlic, onions and peppers for 3 minutes. Add mushrooms and bok choy and sauté for about 5 minutes. Add spinach and adjust seasoning with salt and black pepper.

To prepare red curry sauce, in a small sauté pan over medium heat, warm oil, then sauté onions, garlic, and ginger until golden brown. Add tomato and sauté for another minute. Add cumin, masala, and red curry paste, sauté over low heat for a minute and add coconut milk. Slowly simmer for about 5 minutes or until mixture reaches the consistency of a thick sauce. Just before serving, toss in cilantro and season to taste.

On a warm plate, place vegetables in the center and stack 3 pieces of fried tofu on top.

Crown with red curry sauce and garnish with chives.

Serves 6.

CULINARY NOTES:

Masala is a term used in Indian cuisine to describe a mixture of spices. Most masalas have a foundation of dry spices including garlic, ginger, coriander, cloves, cinnamon and black cardamom. Often-times a masala is sprinkled on top of the finished dish to provide a spicy and pungent aroma.

Ingredients

MARINARA SAUCE

2 tablespoons (30 ml) extra virgin olive oil
1 onion, diced
1 clove garlic, chopped
6 ripe tomatoes, peeled, seeded and diced
1/2 teaspoon (2 g) chopped oregano
1/2 teaspoon (2 g) chopped basil
Salt and freshly ground black pepper

EGGPLANTS

2 to 3 medium eggplant, cut into
1/2-inch thick (1.2 cm) slices (approximately 18)
Salt and freshly ground black pepper
1 cup (250 g) all-purpose flour
2 eggs, beaten
1 cup (250 g) bread crumbs
1 cup (250 ml) vegetable oil

4 tomatoes, sliced 1/2-inch (1.2 cm) thick
(approximately 18 slices)

1 cup (250 g) shredded mozzarella

1/2 cup (120 ml) balsamic vinegar

1 broccoli spear, broken into florettes
4 tablespoons (60 g) unsalted butter

GARNISH

Basil leaves

EGGPLANT MOZZARELLA TOWER

WINE PAIRING – – MERLOT, ARBOLEDA, COLCHAQUA VALLEY, CHILE

Preheat oven to 350°F or 180°C.

For marinara, in a small saucepan over medium heat, warm oil and sauté onion for 4 minutes or until translucent. Add garlic and sauté, stirring continually. Do not brown. Add tomatoes and herbs and season with salt and pepper. Cover and simmer for 10 minutes. Set aside.

Season eggplant slices with salt and pepper, and dredge in flour, shaking off the excess. Next dip each slice in egg, then in the bread crumbs. Set aside.

In a large skillet heat vegetable oil over high heat until very hot. Sauté eggplant one slice at a time until golden brown.

Place the cooked slices on a baking sheet, top each with a tomato slice and sprinkle

with mozzarella. Bake for about 10 minutes, until golden brown and cheese is melted.

In a small saucepan, simmer vinegar until it's reduced by about two-thirds and reaches a syrup consistency. Set aside to cool.

Steam the broccoli florets for 3 minutes. In a small saucepan melt butter. Just before serving, dip the broccoli into butter to coat.

To serve, stack three eggplant/tomato slices on each plate. Garnish with a broccoli floret and basil. Spoon marinara around eggplant tower and drizzle with balsamic reduction.

Serves 6.

CULINARY NOTES:

Most eggplants produce a bitter-tasting alkaloid. A method for removing this unwanted flavor is to sprinkle the slices with salt and let them rest in a colander for an hour. Afterwards, rinse the slices under cold water, gently squeezing out the moisture. Pressing on the slices also collapses the eggplant's air pockets, reducing the absorption of oil during frying.

QUESADILLA

$1/4$ cup (60 ml) extra virgin olive oil
1 small white onion, thickly sliced
1 red bell pepper, thickly sliced
1 yellow bell pepper, thickly sliced
1 green bell pepper, thickly sliced
1 small yellow squash, thickly sliced
2 cloves garlic, minced
Salt and freshly ground black pepper

$1/4$ bunch basil, chopped
$1/4$ bunch oregano, chopped
$1/4$ bunch thyme, chopped
$1/4$ bunch parsley, chopped
3 spinach tortilla wraps (purchased)
$1/4$ cup (60 g) shredded mozzarella
$1/4$ cup (60 g) grated manchego cheese

TOMATO CILANTRO SALSA

1 small red onion, diced
2 small tomatoes, diced
2 small green onions, chopped
$1/2$ bunch cilantro, chopped
1 jalapeño chili, chopped
2 tablespoons (30 ml) salsa picante (purchased)
2 tablespoons (30 ml) freshly squeezed lemon juice
Salt and freshly ground black pepper

GRILLED MEDITERRANEAN
VEGETABLE QUESADILLA

WINE PAIRING – ⍭ – PINOTAGE, FORT SIMON ESTATE, STELLENBOSCH, SOUTH AFRICA

Place oil in a sauté pan, and heat to medium high. Add onion, peppers, squash, and garlic, and cook for 10 minutes or until vegetables are soft. Do not allow garlic to over brown. Season with salt and pepper. Remove from heat and set aside to cool. When cooled, add chopped herbs and blend well.

Preheat oven to 350°F or 180°C.

Place a tortilla on a sheet of plastic wrap, sprinkle the mozzarella on half of the tortilla, layer the vegetable mix on top, and sprinkle with the manchego.

Grease a grill pan and heat to medium high. Fold the tortilla together and place it in the pan, marking each side with grill marks. Place them on a lightly greased sheet pan and heat in the oven for 3 to 4 minutes or until the cheese melts.

To prepare salsa, mix together all ingredients, and season with salt and pepper.

Cut quesadilla in half and place on warm plates.

Serve with guacamole, sour cream, and pickled jalapeño peppers as an accompaniment, if desired.

Serves 6.

CULINARY NOTES:

Most of the heat in the jalapeño comes from the white "ribs" and seeds found inside the peppers. To control the amount of fire in a dish, vary the amount of ribs and seeds you leave when slicing the pepper. Be careful, though. When slicing a pepper never rub your eyes as the oil on your fingers will cause burning and swelling.

PIE CRUST

1 cup (250 g) all-purpose flour
1/2 teaspoon (2 g) salt
1/4 cup (60 g) shortening, room temperature
3 tablespoons (45 ml) water

FILLING

1 tablespoon (15 ml) extra virgin olive oil
1 white onion, small diced
12 asparagus, peeled, blanched and cut into 1/2-inch (1.2 cm) dice
1 tablespoon (15 g) chopped parsley
1 tablespoon (15 g) chopped chives
1/2 tablespoon (10 g) chopped thyme
Salt and freshly ground black pepper
1/3 cup (100 g) shredded Gruyère cheese
8 ounces (230 g) Brie cheese, sliced

3 eggs
1/3 cup (100 ml) heavy cream
Salt and freshly ground black pepper

HERB EMULSION

1 cup (250 g) firmly packed fresh basil leaves (2 bunches)
1/2 bunch chives
1/2 bunch parsley, coarsely chopped
3/4 cup (175 ml) extra virgin olive oil
Salt and freshly ground black pepper

SEMI-DRIED TOMATOES

3 Roma tomatoes, cut in half lengthwise
3 tablespoons (45 ml) garlic oil (purchased)

RED PEPPER REDUCTION

1/2 tablespoon (10 ml) extra virgin olive oil
3 red bell peppers
1/2 teaspoon (2 g) sugar
1 tablespoon (15 ml) Champagne vinegar
2 tablespoons (30 ml) water

BALSAMIC DRESSING

1/4 cup (60 ml) extra virgin olive oil
1/4 cup (60 ml) balsamic vinegar
1 teaspoon (5 g) fresh thyme leaves
Salt and freshly ground black pepper

GARNISH

8 ounce (250 g) arugula

ASPARAGUS AND BRIE TART

Preheat oven to 300°F or 150°C.

In a medium bowl, with a fork, lightly stir together flour and salt. With fork, cut shortening into flour until the mixture resembles coarse crumbs. Sprinkle cold water one teaspoon (5 ml) at a time, mixing lightly with fork after each addition, until pastry begins to hold together. With your hands, shape pastry into a ball. Refrigerate for 30 minutes.

On a lightly floured surface, roll pastry in 1/8-inch (0.3 cm) thick circle about 2-inches (5 cm) larger all around the pie molds.

Roll pastry circle gently onto rolling pin. Transfer to pie molds and unroll. With a sharp knife, trim edges, pinch to form a high edge and make a decorative edge by pressing it with a fork. Prick crusts with a fork to prevent puffing during baking. Refrigerate for 1/2 hour.

Blind bake pie crusts for 5 minutes, remove from oven and let cool.

While crust is baking, warm olive oil in a small saucepan over medium heat, and sauté onions until translucent, about 4 minutes. Add asparagus, fresh herbs, salt and black pepper and sauté for 2 minutes. Do not brown.

Sprinkle tart shells with Gruyère cheese and evenly spread with asparagus mixture.

In a medium bowl, beat eggs lightly, add cream and seasonings. Beat until well mixed.

Pour mixture over cheese and asparagus. Top with sliced Brie. Bake for 20 minutes or until a skewer inserted in the tart comes out clean.

To prepare herb essence, blanch basil and chives in a pan of boiling water for 10 seconds. Drain and refresh in iced water. Pat dry with paper towels and transfer to a blender. Add parsley and oil and purée until smooth. Transfer to a small bowl. Season to taste with salt and pepper and strain using a fine sieve or cheesecloth. Cover and refrigerate until chilled.

Reduce oven to 200°F or 95°C.

Place tomatoes on a small sheet pan, drizzle with garlic oil and bake for 1 hour.

For red pepper reduction, if using a juice extractor, run peppers through your juice extractor. Transfer into a small saucepan, add sugar and vinegar and reduce for 15 minutes, over low heat, until reaching a glaze consistency.

Without a juice extractor, in a small saucepan over medium heat, warm olive oil and sauté sliced peppers for 10 minutes or until soft. Add sugar, vinegar and water and simmer until liquid reduces by half.

Transfer into a blender and purée until smooth. Strain with a cheesecloth and further reduce to a glaze consistency.

For balsamic dressing, in a mixing bowl, combine oil, vinegar, thyme, salt and pepper to taste. Mix well and transfer into a serving dish.

Serve tarts on warmed plates, crown with arugula and semi-dried tomatoes.

Drizzle plate with red pepper reduction and herb essence.

Serves 6.

WHITE SAUCE

2 tablespoons (30 g) butter
4 tablespoons (60 g) flour
1 cup (250 ml) milk
Salt and freshly ground white pepper

FILLING

1/2 onion, finely chopped
1 tablespoon (15 ml) extra virgin olive oil
1 cup (250 g) ricotta cheese
1/4 cup (60 g) grated Parmigiano-Reggiano cheese
1/2 pound (250 g) baby spinach, wilted
Salt and freshly ground black pepper

MARINARA SAUCE

2 tablespoons (30 ml) extra virgin olive oil
1 onion, diced
3 cloves garlic, chopped
6 ripe tomatoes, peeled, seeded and diced
1/2 teaspoon (2 g) chopped basil
Salt and freshly ground black pepper

MELANZANE

2 medium size eggplants, skinned and thinly sliced lengthwise
1/4 cup (60 g) flour
2 tablespoons (30 ml) extra virgin olive oil
1/4 cup (60 g) grated Parmigiano-Reggiano cheese

HERBED OIL

1/4 bunch basil
1/4 bunch parsley
1/4 bunch chives
1/2 cup (120 ml) extra virgin olive oil

GARNISH

12 shavings Parmigiano-Reggiano cheese
Fried basil leaves

MELANZANE RIPIENI DI RICOTTA E SPINACI ALLA PARMIGIANA
Eggplant roulades filled with ricotta and spinach, Parmesan style

Preheat oven to 350°F or 180°C.

For white sauce, in a small stockpot, melt butter over medium heat; gradually add flour a spoonful at a time to create a roux. Cook over medium heat for 2 to 3 minutes. Do not brown. Slowly whisk in milk. Bring to a boil and stir consistently to avoid lumps. Season with salt and pepper.

In a small sauté pan over medium heat, sauté onions in oil for 3 minutes or until translucent. Add ricotta, season with salt and pepper and cook for 10 minutes. Combine with white sauce and Parmesan cheese.

In a sauté pan over medium heat, place spinach and pan-fry for 5 minutes. Season and squeeze all the water out of them. Add to ricotta mixture. Mix well and let cool.

For marinara, in a small saucepan over medium heat, warm oil and sauté onion and garlic for 4 minutes or until onions are translucent. Add tomatoes and herbs and season with salt and pepper. Cover and simmer for 10 minutes. Set aside.

Toss eggplant slices in flour. Shake well to remove excess flour. In a frying pan over high heat, warm oil and fry eggplants 1 minute on each side. Set aside on a plate layered with absorbent paper.

On a lightly greased sheet pan, lay eggplant slices and fill with ricotta mixture. Roll and top with some marinara sauce, sprinkle with Parmesan cheese and bake for 10 minutes.

To prepare herbed oil, blanch herbs in a pan of boiling water for 10 seconds. Drain and refresh in iced water. Pat dry with paper and transfer to a blender. Add oil and purée until smooth. Using a fine sieve or cheesecloth, strain into a small bowl. Cover and set aside.

To serve, place a couple spoonfuls of marinara in the center of each warmed plate. Top with 2 eggplant rolls and the wilted spinach. Garnish with Parmesan shavings and fried basil. Finish with herbed oil drizzles.

Serves 6.

CULINARY NOTES:

You will want to purchase whole, solid Parmigiano-Reggiano cheese and grate or shave your own. The grated kind in the thin green tube is just not the same.

"Parmesan" is a common term for any cheese imitating true grana-style cheeses.

Grana-style cheese is a hard granular cheese that is cooked but not pressed. It is made from raw milk and aged for up to 12 months. Only milk produced from May 1 to November 11 is used in producing the true Parmigiano-Reggiano cheese.

VEGETABLE CURRY

2 tablespoons (30 ml) vegetable oil

2 tablespoons (30 g) peeled, minced fresh ginger

2 cloves garlic, minced

1 pound (450 g) Spanish onions cut into $^1/_4$-inch (0.6 cm) slices

1 teaspoon (5 g) curry powder

1 teaspoon (5 g) ground cumin

1 teaspoon (5 g) ground coriander

1 teaspoon (5 g) cayenne powder

1 teaspoon (5 g) ground turmeric

1 bay leaf

$^1/_2$ pound (250 g) carrots, peeled and cut into $^1/_2$-inch (1.2 cm) cubes

$^3/_4$ pound (350 g) potatoes, peeled and cut into $^1/_2$-inch (1.2 cm) cubes

$^1/_4$ pound (120 g) eggplant, cut into $^1/_2$-inch (1.2 cm) cubes

$1^1/_2$ quarts (1.5 L) vegetable stock (page 158)

$^1/_4$ pound (120 g) cauliflower florets

1 pound (450 g) Roma tomatoes, cut into $^1/_2$-inch (1.2 cm) slices

$^1/_4$ pound (120 g) frozen okra, sliced (keep frozen until ready to use)

$^1/_4$ bunch cilantro

1 pound (450 g) frozen peas

3 ounces (100 g) plain yogurt

Salt and freshly ground black pepper

JASMINE RICE

$1^1/_2$ cups (400 g) Jasmine rice

$1^1/_2$ cups (400 ml) cold water

6 (7-inch) (18 cm) flour tortillas, purchased

CUCUMBER RAITA

1 pound (450 g) cucumbers, peeled in alternate strips, seeded and grated

$^1/_2$ cup (120 g) plain yogurt

1 tomato, peeled, seeded and cut into $^1/_8$-inch (0.3 cm) cubes

$^1/_4$ bunch mint, chopped

GARNISH

Pappadam, purchased

Fresh chervil

INDIAN VEGETABLE CURRY

WINE PAIRING – – VIOGNIER, BERINGER, NAPA VALLEY, CALIFORNIA

For curry, in a large sauté pan, heat oil over medium heat and add ginger, garlic, onions and all the spices. Sauté for about 5 minutes, until the onions are light blond and soft. Do not brown.

Add carrots, potatoes, and eggplant, and sauté for about 10 minutes.

Add vegetable stock, stir and bring to a boil. Add cauliflower, tomatoes, frozen okra, and cilantro. Stir, cover and turn heat down to medium low. Simmer for 10 minutes and add frozen peas. Simmer for another 5 minutes or until all the vegetables are soft. Adjust seasoning with salt and pepper.

Just before serving swirl in yogurt.

Rinse rice with cold water 3 to 4 times or until water runs clear. Drain one last time.

Place rice in a pot; add water, let stand for 30 minutes, and bring to a boil. The liquid should be 1 inch (2.5 cm) above the rice. Cook, covered, for 15 minutes. Remove rice from heat, and keep covered on the side of stove for 20 minutes.

Preheat oven to 350°F or 180°C.

Place each tortilla in 4 inch (10 cm) ramekins and bake for 10 minutes or until lightly browned and set.

To prepare raita, mix cucumber, yogurt, tomato and mint.

On a warm plate, place tortilla shell in the center and fill with curry. Serve with rice, raita and pappadam. Garnish with chervil.

Serves 6.

CULINARY NOTES:

How to peel ginger: If you use a knife to remove the skin from a piece of ginger you will find that a good portion of the ginger root comes off with the skin. Try using a spoon to scrape the skin away from the root. The skin is very thin and will come away with a few scrapes. You will also be able to use the tip of the spoon to get into all the little cracks and crevices.

Designed to recognize creativity aboard the world's leading cruise and ferry lines, the BACARDI® Cruise Competition calls for bartenders and chefs to create recipes incorporating and drawing inspiration from BACARDI® products.

Cruise line bartenders and chefs from twenty-two cruise and ferry lines are invited to create inspired new cocktails and culinary recipes using world-class products such as BACARDI® rums, BOMBAY SAPPHIRE® gin, to name only a few as well as liqueurs like DRAMBUIE® and DISARONNO®.

Recipes are judged by Johnson & Wales University, the Show Tenders and a VIP panel comprised of cruise line executives, culinary experts, cocktail specialists and press. The highest rated cocktail and culinary recipes are awarded the Bacardi Bartender of the Year and Bacardi Chef of the Year honors as well as a cash scholarship for independent study.

For the past two years, Royal Caribbean International has taken part and won in the BACARDI® "Bartender & Chef" Cruise Competition creating mouth-watering recipes such as the ones presented in this chapter.

BACARDI.

SAUCE

2 tablespoons (30 g) butter
2 shallots, finely chopped
1/2 cup (120 ml) Martini & Rossi® dry vermouth
1/2 cup (120 ml) white wine
1 cup (250 ml) fish stock (page 158)
10 threads saffron, soaked in 1/8 cup (30 ml) of warm water
1 1/2 cups (350 ml) heavy cream
1/3 teaspoon (1 ml) Worcestershire sauce
Salt and freshly ground white pepper

PASTA

1 pound (450 g) dry tagliatelli pasta
1 teaspoon (5 ml) extra virgin olive oil

SEAFOOD

3 (6 to 7-ounce) (200 g) lobster tails
Salt and freshly ground white pepper
2 tablespoons (30 ml) extra virgin olive oil

1 tablespoon (15 ml) extra virgin olive oil
1 clove garlic, finely chopped
12 large size shrimp, peeled, deveined, and tails left on (size 16/20)
Juice of 1/2 lemon
Salt and freshly ground white pepper

12 sea scallops
Salt and freshly ground white pepper
1 tablespoon (15 ml) extra virgin olive oil

1 teaspoon (5 ml) extra virgin olive oil
1 clove garlic, finely chopped
1 shallot, finely chopped
1 cup (250 ml) dry white wine
2 dozen fresh mussels, scrubbed and rinsed
Salt and freshly ground black pepper

GARNISH

1/4 bunch chives, chopped
1 red chili pepper, deseeded and finely chopped

Guenther Bartschte,
Senior Executive Chef, CEC

Chef Guenther started his culinary career in 1984 training in various hotels and restaurants in Germany and Switzerland.

He started working on cruise ships in 1991 for Crystal Cruises and roamed the high seas for a while before establishing himself in Munich working as an Executive Chef for the then famous restaurant "Mangostin Asia."

His love of travel made him move to Russia, the Middle East and various countries in Europe delighting guests at the Sheraton Hotels with his culinary delicacies.

Chef Guenther came back to the cruise industry in 2000 and has been with Royal Caribbean International since then.

When not on board, Chef Guenther likes skiing and traveling around the world visiting friends and family.

"TREASURE OF THE SEA" TAGLIATELLI

Preheat oven to 450°F or 230°C.

For sauce, in a small saucepan over medium heat, melt butter and sauté shallots for 3 minutes until translucent. Deglaze with Martini & Rossi®; add wine and fish stock and simmer for 10 minutes or until sauce is reduced by half. Add saffron threads, cream and Worcestershire sauce, adjust seasoning with salt and pepper and simmer for 10 minutes or until sauce is thick enough to coat the back of a spoon. Do not boil. Keep warm.

Cook pasta in a stockpot of boiling salted water until al dente, about 8 to 10 minutes. Drain well and toss with olive oil.

With a sharp knife, cut lobster tail shells down the soft underside to expose the flesh. Devein and partially lift meat from shell. Season with salt and pepper and brush with olive oil. Broil lobsters in oven for 6 to 8 minutes until the tail meat is white. Keep warm.

In a sauté pan over high heat, warm oil and sauté garlic and shrimp for 5 to 7 minutes until shrimp are pink. Season with salt and pepper, and finish with lemon juice. Set aside.

Pat dry and season scallops with salt and pepper. In a sauté pan, over medium heat, warm oil and sauté scallops, in batches, until firm and opaque, about 2 minutes on each side. Keep warm.

In a small stockpot, warm oil over medium heat and sauté garlic and shallots for 3 minutes, until translucent. Deglaze with wine, add mussels, cover and steam for 5 minutes or until mussels are open, shaking pot occasionally. Season with salt and pepper. Discard any mussels that do not open. Remove mussels from shells and set aside.

Add pasta to sauce. Toss to coat and serve in warmed deep plates. Arrange seafood on pasta and garnish with chopped chives and red chili pepper.

Serves 6.

SIMPLE SEAFOOD BROTH

SEAFOOD

1 tablespoon (15 ml) extra virgin olive oil
2 cloves garlic, minced
12 large size shrimp, peeled, deveined, and tails left on (size 16/20)
12 sea scallops (size 10/20)
2 dozen fresh mussels, scrubbed and rinsed

2 tablespoons (30 ml) Martini & Rossi® dry vermouth
4 cups (1 L) fish stock (page 158)
1/3 teaspoon (1 g) chili flakes
1/4 bunch parsley, minced
1 teaspoon (5 g) minced thyme leaves
6 (3-ounce) (85 g) salmon fillets, skinned

1 onion, julienned
1 carrot, julienned
2 stalks celery, julienned
Salt and freshly ground black pepper

GARNISH

Alfalfa sprouts

SIMPLE SEAFOOD BROTH
Ramesh Thirumal, Sous Chef

In a saucepan over medium heat, warm oil and sauté garlic for 2 minutes. Do not brown. Add shrimp, scallops and mussels and sauté for 2 to 3 minutes.

Deglaze with vermouth, moisten with stock, add chili flakes and herbs and bring to a boil.

Add salmon fillets and julienned vegetables, season with salt and pepper and cook for 5 minutes.

Before serving, discard any mussels that have not opened.

Ladle soup into heated bowls and garnish with alfalfa sprouts.

Serves 6.

POACHED HALIBUT WITH BACARDI® COCO BUTTER SAUCE

VEGETABLES

1 bok choy, trimmed, spears separated from root
18 asparagus spears
1 carrot, peeled, julienned
1 leek, julienned

CRAB MOUSSE

1 tablespoon (15 g) butter
1 tablespoon (15 ml) vegetable oil
1 clove garlic, minced
1 white onion, finely chopped

8 oz (250 g) crab meat
1/4 cup (60 ml) Martini & Rossi® Asti
1/2 cup (120 ml) heavy cream
2 egg whites
Salt and freshly ground white pepper

FISH

6 (5-ounce or 150 g) halibut fillets, sliced horizontally
Salt and freshly ground white pepper
Juice of 1 lemon

4 cups (1 L) hot fish stock (page 158)

BEURRE BLANC

2 shallots, minced
6 black peppercorns, crushed
1/3 cup (90 ml) Bacardi® Coco flavored rum
1/2 cup (120 ml) heavy cream
1/2 pound (250 g) unsalted butter, room temperature

GARNISH

3 tablespoons (45 g) shredded coconut, roasted

POACHED HALIBUT WITH BACARDI® COCO BUTTER SAUCE
George Santos, Commis Chef

Preheat oven to 350°F or 180°C.

Blanch bok choy in boiling salted water for 8 minutes. Remove from boiling water, cool in ice, drain and set aside. Return salted water to a boil, blanch asparagus for 5 minutes, Cool in ice, drain and set aside. Repeat operation for carrot and leek julienne.

To prepare mousse, in a sauté pan over medium heat, warm butter and oil and sauté garlic and onion for 3 minutes or until translucent. Add crab meat and deglaze with Asti wine. Simmer for 5 minutes. Transfer mixture into a food processor;

add cream, egg whites and seasoning and blend until smooth. Spoon mousse into a piping bag and set aside.

Pat-dry fish, season with salt and pepper and rub with lemon juice.

Place bottom half fish into a baking pan, pipe in crab mousse, top with remaining fish slice and wrap each fish parcel with bok choy leaves.

Pour in fish stock and cover with aluminum foil. Bake for 20 minutes.

Meanwhile, combine shallots, peppercorns and rum in a saucepan. Simmer for 5 minutes over

medium heat or until sauce liquids have reduced by 70 percent. Add cream and slow cook for 10 minutes. Do not boil. Remove from heat and whisk in butter a little at a time. Strain through a sieve. Keep warm.

Reheat asparagus and julienne vegetables separately in hot water.

To serve, place fish in the center of warmed plate, top with asparagus and a mound of julienned vegetables. Finish with sauce and a sprinkling of roasted coconut.

Serves 6.

*Our dessert complemented
the design of our meal and
left a lasting impression
of true elegance.*

DESSERTS

CROQUANT
3/4 cup (150 g) macadamia nuts
1/2 cup (120 g) sugar
2 tablespoons (30 ml) water
1 teaspoon (5 ml) vegetable oil

PARFAIT
4 eggs
6 egg yolks
1 cup (250 g) sugar
2 cups (500 ml) heavy cream

CARAMEL SAUCE
1 cup (250 g) sugar
1/3 cup (90 ml) water
1/2 tablespoon (7.5 g) unsalted butter
1/2 cup (120 ml) vanilla ice cream

GARNISH
Chocolate sauce, purchased, warmed

BANANA AND CRUNCHY NUT PARFAIT

Preheat oven to 375°F or 190°C.

For croquant, place macadamia nuts on a sheet pan and toast for 7 minutes or until lightly browned.

Mix sugar and water in a small pan and simmer until golden brown. Add nuts to caramel and stir to coat. Grease a baking sheet and pour caramel and nuts onto it. Allow the mixture to cool.

For the parfait, using an electric mixer, whisk eggs, egg yolks and 3/4 cup (150g) sugar together until doubled in volume.

In another bowl, using an electric mixer, beat cream and remaining sugar until soft peaks form.

Gently fold the two mixtures together. Crush caramel-nut croquant and stir into mixture. Pour into a parchment paper-lined terrine mold. Place terrine in freezer for at least 3 hours.

For caramel sauce, melt sugar and water in a small saucepan over medium heat and simmer until golden brown. Remove from heat, add butter, and slowly mix in ice cream.

Remove parfait from mold by warming sides under hot running water.

Slice parfait and serve on chilled plates. Drizzle with chocolate sauce and caramel sauce.

Serves 10.

CULINARY NOTES:

Croquant is a fancy French name for nut brittle. Once the sugar and nut mixture has cooled completely, break up into small pieces using a rolling pin or plastic cup.

For an equally fancy garnish, prepare a batch of the macadamia nut croquant and allow it to cool to the touch.

Working quickly, slice or cut several shapes and wrap or lay them across a variety of surfaces, spoons, rolling pins, etc. The cooled shapes will then be able to stand upright and retain whatever shape they are in.

CRÈME BRÛLÉE

2 cups (450 ml) heavy cream
4 egg yolks
$^{1}/_{2}$ cup (100 g) sugar
$^{1}/_{2}$ ripe banana, puréed
1 shot Bailey's® Irish Cream

CARAMELIZED BANANAS

2 tablespoons (30 g) butter
2 tablespoons (30 g) sugar
6 small bananas

GARNISH

$^{1}/_{4}$ cup (60 g) brown sugar
6 Sugar moons (purchased)
1 cup (250 g) assorted berries
Mint leaves

BAILEY'S® BANANA BRÛLÉE

Preheat oven to 350°F or 180°C.

In a saucepan over medium heat, slowly bring cream to a boil.

In a mixing bowl, combine egg yolks and sugar and beat until mixture is lemon colored. Place over simmering water and beat until mixture has doubled in volume, about 10 minutes.

Remove from heat and keep whisking to cool it down.

Slowly stir hot cream and Bailey's® into egg mixture. Using a fine sieve, strain into a bowl set over ice to quickly chill the mixture. Add puréed banana and mix well.

Pour mixture into individual molds set in a shallow pan or baking dish. Pour water into the pan until it is half way up the sides of the molds and bake for 40 minutes.

To make bananas, melt butter and sugar in a small sauté pan over medium heat. Add bananas and caramelize on all sides for a total of 2 minutes. Do not brown.

Evenly sprinkle top with brown sugar and place under broiler or use a pastry blow torch to heat sugar until it turns brown and bubbles.

Let set for a few minutes, then garnish with caramelized banana, Sugar moons, berries and mint.

Serves 6.

CULINARY NOTES:

Set the crème brûlée molds in a shallow pan or baking dish and place in the oven. Then pour warm water around the molds. This avoids spilling water on the floor or into the custard when placing the pan in the oven.

The water surrounds the molds and creates a thermal "jacket" around the custard as it bakes. As the water heats, it keeps the custard at an even temperature and helps the custard set evenly.

CHOCOLATE CAKE

1 1/2 cups (370 g) semisweet chocolate
1 cup (250 g) unsalted butter
5 eggs
5 egg yolks
3/4 cup (150 g) flour, sifted
2 tablespoons (30 ml) brandy

BRANDY SNAP

1 1/4 cups (310 g) sugar
3/4 cup (150 g) unsalted butter
3/4 cup (150 g) all-purpose flour, sifted
3/4 cup (175 ml) corn syrup

GARNISH

2 pears
2 teaspoons (10 g) granulated sugar
1/4 cup (60 ml) chocolate sauce,
purchased, warmed
Vanilla bean ice cream, purchased
Mint leaves
1 tablespoon (15 g) cocoa powder

WARM CHOCOLATE PUDDING

Preheat oven to 300°F or 150°C.

Grease ramekins or individual molds.

In a double boiler, melt chocolate and butter. Do not over heat. Remove from heat and let cool.

Using an electric mixer, whisk eggs and egg yolks until well mixed. Gently stir chocolate mixture into eggs.

Fold in sifted flour, then add brandy.

Pour into molds and bake for 22 minutes.

For the Brandy Snap, combine all ingredients and refrigerate for 1 hour. Roll out to 1/4-inch (.62 cm) flat on a sheet of parchment paper. Bake for about 30 minutes or until golden brown. While still warm, cut into 2-inch by 2-inch (5 x 5 cm) wide squares.

Peel and thinly slice pear, coat with sugar and roast in oven for 2 minutes.

Place individual warm cakes in the center of plates, coat with chocolate sauce, and top with Brandy Snap squares and roasted pear slices, fanned out. Garnish with a scoop of ice cream and mint leaf. Sprinkle with cocoa powder.

Serves 8.

CHOCA-CHINO TRILOGY

WHITE CHOCOLATE MOUSSE

WHITE CHOCOLATE MOUSSE
1/2 cup (100 g) white chocolate
3 tablespoons (45 g) butter
1/2 cup (120 ml) heavy cream

5 eggs, yolks and whites separated
1/2 cup (100 g) sugar
1 tablespoon (15 ml) Grand Marnier®

1 cup (250 ml) heavy cream, whipped

GARNISH
32 raspberries
8 chocolate triangles (purchased)
Orange zest

In a small saucepan over low heat, warm chocolate, butter and cream until chocolate has melted. Stir to combine and set aside.

In a small mixing bowl, beat egg yolks with 1/2 the sugar and Grand Marnier®; blanch using an electric mixer at high speed for about 5 minutes or until mixture is frothy.

Slowly incorporate to chocolate mixture.

In a mixing bowl, beat egg whites with an electric mixer on medium speed until frothy. Increase speed to high and gradually add sugar, beating eggs until they form soft peaks. Fold in chocolate mixture and whipped cream.

Cover and refrigerate for 24 hours.

To serve, using a soup spoon dipped in warm water, delicately scoop a spoonful of chocolate mousse and place atop chocolate triangle and raspberries.

Garnish with orange zest.

Serves 8.

MUD CAKE

MUD CAKE ICING
1 pound (450 g) dark chocolate
2 cups (500 ml) heavy cream

MUD CAKE
1 pound (450 g) flour, sifted
1 1/4 pounds (570 g) sugar
1/4 teaspoon (1 g) salt
1/2 teaspoon (2 g) baking powder

1/2 teaspoon (2 g) baking soda
1/3 cup (90 g) cocoa powder
1 teaspoon (5 g) coffee powder
3 eggs
1 teaspoon (5 ml) vanilla extract
1/2 cup (120 ml) vegetable oil
1 1/2 cups (370 ml) sour cream
1 cup (250 ml) water

GARNISH
Apricot sauce (purchased)
Raspberry sauce (purchased)

Preheat oven to 400°F or 200°C.

In a small saucepan over low heat, warm chocolate and cream until chocolate has melted. Stir well and transfer into a stainless steel bowl; cover and refrigerate for 24 hours.

For mud cake, using an electric mixer at medium speed, mix all ingredients together for approximately 4 minutes. Transfer batter into a prepared 8-inch

(20.5 cm) cake pan. Bake for 35 minutes or until a skewer inserted in cake comes out clean.

Remove cake from oven and allow cooling to room temperature in pan. Transfer to a wire rack with a matching size sheet pan underneath and, with a serrated knife, slice off the middle top of the cake and spread the bottom with a fine coat (1/2-inch or 1 cm) of cold mud icing. Place top back on.

In a small saucepan over low heat, warm 1/2 of the remaining icing (the rest will be used to make the Kahlúa cheesecake). Evenly spread over the cake top and sides. Refrigerate.

Cut cake into triangles. Drizzle sauces on plate and gently arrange chocolate triangle with the point facing up.

Serves 8.

CHOCOLATE KAHLÚA® CHEESECAKE

FILLING
*1¼ pounds (570 g) cream cheese, room
temperature*
¼ cup (60 g) sugar
5 egg yolks
¾ cup (150 ml) sour cream
3 tablespoons (45 ml) Kahlúa®
Remaining mud cake icing

DARK CHOCOLATE CHANTILLY
¼ cup (60 ml) heavy cream
*¼ cup (60 ml) dark chocolate
sauce (purchased)*

GARNISH
8 chocolate butterflies (purchased)

Preheat oven to 400°F or 200°C.

In a mixing bowl, mix cream cheese and
sugar and beat at medium speed,
occasionally scraping down the sides of
the bowl until fully mixed. Switch speed to
low and add eggs one at a time until fully
mixed. Add sour cream, Kahlúa® and cold
mud cake icing. Mix well. Pour mixture

into prepared individual molds. Bake for
45 minutes or until edges are set and
center is firm. Remove cheesecakes from
oven and let cool. Cover with a plastic
wrap and refrigerate for at least
2 hours.

In a small mixing bowl over high speed,
beat heavy cream until it forms soft peaks.

Fold in chocolate sauce and refrigerate.

Before serving, finish each Kahlúa®
cheesecake by piping dark chocolate
chantilly atop cakes in the form of a
rosette and garnish with a chocolate
butterfly.

Serves 8.

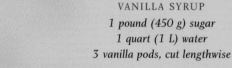

VANILLA SYRUP
1 pound (450 g) sugar
1 quart (1 L) water
3 vanilla pods, cut lengthwise

PINEAPPLE
2 golden pineapples
12 vanilla pods

GARNISH
$1/4$ cup (60 ml) whipped cream
Candied cherries, purchased

Robert Mead, Corporate Pastry Chef

Chef Robert joined Royal Caribbean International in January 2005. Robert was born in Sydney, Australia. From an early age Robert was inspired by the sweet creations from his grandmother's kitchen. Robert went on to complete his training in a small patisserie, finishing "Most Outstanding Student" in his year. Upon completion of his training Robert started his own pastry adventure, taking him to all corners of the globe in search of perfect sweet endings. Robert has a keen interest in sports, along with a passion for travel. He enjoys artistic ventures in his spare time.

VANILLA ROASTED SWEET PINEAPPLE

Preheat oven to 400°F or 200°C.

Prepare syrup by mixing all ingredients in a saucepan and boiling until sugar is melted.

With a sharp knife, slice pineapple in half lengthwise, and then cut into quarters. Peel and cut out the core. Pass vanilla pods through the quarters with a large needle.

Poach pineapple quarters for 5 minutes in the syrup, then transfer to a baking sheet and roast for 15 minutes, until the pineapple quarters are nicely golden.

To serve, place 2 pieces of pineapple on each plate, and garnish with a dollop of whipped cream and a cherry.

Serves 6.

POACHED PEARS

1 3/4 cups (400 g) sugar
1 quart (1 L) water
2 tablespoons (30 g) peeled, chopped ginger
6 pears, peeled and cored

1 tablespoon (15 g) butter
2 tablespoons (30 g) sugar

CHOCOLATE TRUFFLES

1/2 cup (120 g) semisweet chocolate
1/4 cup (60 g) unsweetened chocolate
5 egg yolks
1/2 cup (120 g) sugar
1/4 cup (60 g) finely chopped galangal
2 cups (450 g) heavy cream
1 tablespoon (15 g) unsalted butter

1/4 cup (60 g) cocoa powder

CARAMEL LICHEES

1 cup (250 g) sugar
1/4 cup (60 ml) water
1/4 cup (60 ml) whiskey
1 mango, peeled and diced
1 (8-ounce) (240 g) can lichees

GARNISH
Mint leaves

ASIAN POACHED PEARS WITH CHOCOLATE TRUFFLES AND CARAMEL LICHEES

In a saucepan combine sugar, water, and ginger and bring to a boil. Add pears and simmer for 8 minutes, or until pears are tender. Remove from heat, cover, and refrigerate.

In a double boiler over hot water, melt chocolates.

In a mixing bowl, combine egg yolks and sugar and beat until the mixture is lemon colored. Fold in chocolate and stir in galangal.

In a stainless steel bowl, beat cream until it forms soft peaks. Fold into chocolate mixture.

With buttered hands, shape mixture into 1-inch (2.5 cm) balls. Place balls on a sheet pan lined with parchment paper and

freeze for 1 hour. Roll each ball in cocoa powder and refrigerate until serving.

For caramel lichees, in a saucepan over low heat, melt sugar and water and simmer until golden. Remove from heat and whisk in the whiskey very slowly. Add the mango and lichees and place back on the stove, simmering for 5 minutes.

To finish pears, warm a sauté pan over medium heat, and melt the butter. Sprinkle pears with sugar and sauté on all sides for 2 minutes until nicely golden.

Arrange pears on plates, top with a mint leaf, and spoon some caramelized lichees around them. Place a couple truffles on the plate and serve immediately.

Serves 6.

Romeo Bueno, Corporate Pastry Chef

Chef Romeo joined Royal Caribbean International in 1981 as an Executive Pastry Chef and has served as a Pastry Supervisor with the company since 1995. Hailing from Manila, Philippines, Romeo completed his pastry apprenticeship, then commenced his career at The Manila Royal Hotel as an Assistant Pastry Cook. Romeo also served at the 5-star Makati Executive Centre Hotel as the Executive Pastry Chef. Chef Romeo began his quest for international experience with Disney Cruise Lines as an Executive Pastry Chef. Romeo makes his home with his wife Eleonor and children Nicolo and Nicaella in the town of Rizal, Cainta, Philippines.

CRUST

1/2 cup (120 g) unsalted butter, melted
1 1/2 cups (350 g) Oreo® cookie crumbs

FILLING

2 pounds (900 g) cream cheese, softened
3/4 cup (150 g) sugar
1/3 cup (90 g) flour
3 egg yolks
1/2 cup (120 ml) heavy cream

1 teaspoon (5 ml) vanilla extract
1 pound (450 g) Oreo® cookies, crushed

MERINGUE

3 egg whites
1/4 cup (60 g) sugar

BERRY COMPOTE

1 cup (250 g) raspberries
1 cup (250 g) blackberries
1 cup (250 g) strawberries
1/2 cup (120 g) blueberries

1/3 cup (90 g) sugar
1 teaspoon (5 g) lemon zest
1/4 cup (60 ml) water

GARNISH

Powdered sugar
Mint leaves
10 chocolate twigs (purchased)

OREO® CHEESECAKE

Preheat oven to 300°F or 150°C.

For crust, pour melted butter over Oreo® crumbs and mix. Strongly press mixture into the bottom of a cheesecake or springform cake pan in an even layer. Bake for 10 minutes.

To make filling, in a mixing bowl, mix cream cheese and sugar and beat at medium speed until smooth. Add flour and beat well, occasionally scraping down the sides of the bowl until fully incorporated. Add egg yolks and heavy cream. Beat until mixture is light and fluffy.

For meringue, using an electric mixer on medium speed, beat egg whites and a pinch of salt until eggs are frothy. Increase speed to high and gradually incorporate sugar, beating egg whites until they form soft peaks.

Fold egg white meringue into cream cheese filling and gently mix until the batter is light and airy. Fold in vanilla extract and Oreo® crumbs.

Pour mixture into cake pan. Bake for 1 hour 15 minutes or until edges are set and center is firm.

Remove cheesecake from oven and allow to cool. Cover with plastic wrap and refrigerate for at least 2 hours.

For berry compote, mix all ingredients in a small saucepan and simmer for 5 minutes or until berries are ready to burst. Remove from heat, transfer into a stainless steel bowl, cover and refrigerate for 2 hours.

Upon serving, sprinkle cheesecake slices with powdered sugar and garnish with a spoonful of berry compote, mint leaves and a chocolate stick.

Serves 10.

Dolcetti Alla Portofino

Tiramisù

TIRAMISÙ
3 egg yolks
2 tablespoons (30 g) sugar

3/4 cup (150 g) Mascarpone cheese at room temperature
2 tablespoons (30 ml) amaretto

1/4 cup (60 ml) heavy cream

3 egg whites
2 tablespoons (30 g) sugar

1 leaf of gelatin (purchased)
1/4 cup (60 ml) lukewarm water

3 tablespoons (45 ml) Kahlúa®
3 tablespoons (45 ml) espresso coffee or strong brewed coffee
8 ladyfingers

GARNISH
Cocoa powder, for dusting

In a medium bowl mix egg yolks and sugar; blanch using an electric mixer at high speed for about 5 minutes or until mixture is frothy. Place bowl over a pot of simmering water and whisk, at medium speed for 10 more minutes or until mixture has doubled in volume. Remove from heat.

In a bowl break up Mascarpone, add amaretto, and whisk until well blended.

In a chilled mixing bowl, whip heavy cream into stiff peaks and fold into Mascarpone mixture.

Beat egg whites with sugar until stiff.

Soften gelatin in water. Remove from water and slowly fold into the lukewarm egg yolk mixture. Gently fold egg yolks and Mascarpone mixtures into egg whites.

In a separate bowl mix Kahlúa® and espresso coffee. Cut ladyfingers in half, across, and soak in espresso mixture.

Place 2 pieces of soaked lady fingers in the bottom of shot glasses and top with Mascarpone cream. Chill for 2 hours or until set.

To serve, dust tiramisù cups with cocoa powder.

Serves 8.

Flourless Chocolate Cake

3/4 cup (150 g) semisweet chocolate chips
3/4 cup (150 g) unsalted butter

4 eggs
1/2 cup (120 g) sugar
1 tablespoon (15 ml) dark rum
1/2 tablespoon (7.5 ml) vanilla extract
1/3 cup (90 ml) strong brewed coffee

CHOCOLATE WAFFLES
3/4 cup (150 g) semisweet chocolate chips
Bubble wrap

GARNISH
Whipped cream

Preheat the oven to 300°F or 150°C.

Place chocolate and butter in the top of a double boiler set over 1 inch (2.5 cm) of simmering water. Whisk until chocolate is smooth. Set aside to cool, stirring continuously.

Using an electric mixer beat eggs and sugar until creamy. Gradually fold chocolate into egg mixture, add rum, vanilla extract and coffee and mix well.

Bring a large kettle of water to a boil.

Pour mixture into prepared 8-inch (20 cm) pan or 8 individual molds and cover with aluminum foil. Place in a roasting pan and pour in enough boiling water to come halfway up the outside of the pan. Bake for 30 minutes or until a skewer inserted comes out clean.

Remove cake (s) from oven and allow cooling to room temperature in pan. Transfer to a wire rack and chill overnight.

For chocolate waffles, place chocolate in the top of a double boiler set over 1 inch (2.5 cm) of simmering water. Whisk until chocolate is smooth. Spread over bubble wrap and allow to cool. Refrigerate for 1 hour. Remove bubble wrap and cut into triangles.

Cut cake as desired if necessary. Pipe a rosette of whipped cream atop each cake and garnish with a chocolate waffle.

Serves 8.

PANNA COTTA

1 gelatin leaf (purchased)
1/4 cup (60 g) strawberry jelly
4 egg whites
1 cup (250 ml) milk
2 cups (450 ml) heavy cream
1/4 cup (60 g) sugar
2 tablespoons (30 g) powdered pistachio

GARNISH
Unsalted pistachios, chopped

Place gelatin leaf in a bowl of warm water to soften. Layer bottom of ramekins with strawberry jelly.

In a small bowl, using an electric mixer, whisk egg whites until soft peaks form.

In a saucepan, over low heat, warm milk, cream, sugar and pistachio. Remove from heat and fold in softened gelatin. Cool, stirring constantly, for 5 to 7 minutes. Gently mix with egg white mixture and pour into individual molds. Refrigerate for 3 hours.

Upon serving, remove from mold and garnish with pistachios.

Serves 8.

WHITE CHOCOLATE POT DE CRÈME

1/4 cup (60 g) white chocolate chips
2 eggs
1/4 cup (60 g) sugar
1 cup (250 ml) milk

GARNISH
Mint leaves
Chocolate sticks, purchased
Chocolate triangles, purchased

Preheat the oven to 300°F or 150°C.

Place chocolate in the top of a double boiler set over 1 inch (2.5 cm) of simmering water. Whisk until chocolate is smooth.

Prepare crème by creaming eggs with sugar. Bring milk to a boil, and slowly stir into egg mixture. Add melted chocolate and pour mixture into individual molds set in a shallow pan or baking dish. Cover with aluminum paper. Pour hot water into pan until it is half way up the sides of the molds and bake for 20 minutes. Refrigerate for 2 hours.

Garnish with a chocolate stick and a chocolate triangle. Finish with mint leaves.

Serves 8.

SHORTBREAD CRUST

1 1/2 cups (370 g) flour
3/4 cup (150 g) sugar
3 tablespoons (45 g) cornstarch
1 pinch salt
1 tablespoon (15 g) lemon zest
1 cup unsalted butter (1 1/2 sticks or 250 g),
cut into 1/2-inch (1.2 cm) pieces

FILLING

1 (16-ounce) (500 g) can peaches,
drained and sliced
1 (16-ounce) (500 g) can apples, drained
and sliced
1/4 cup (60 g) sugar
1 teaspoon (5 g) cinnamon powder
1/4 cup (60 g) raisins

CRUMBLES

1 1/2 cups (370 g) flour
1 cup (250 g) sugar
1/2 cup (120 g) unsalted butter,
room temperature
or
1 vanilla sponge cake mix, purchased, baked as
per recipe and crumbled

CRÈME ANGLAISE

2 egg yolks
1/4 cup (60 g) sugar
1 cup (250 ml) milk
1 teaspoon (5 g) orange zest

ROASTED PEACHES

1 tablespoon (15 g) unsalted butter
1 tablespoon (15 g) sugar
5 fresh peaches, halved

GARNISH

Cinnamon powder
10 scoops vanilla ice cream
1/4 cup (60 g) slivered almonds, roasted

APPLE-PEACH CRUMBLE

Preheat oven to 300°F or 150°C.

To make crust, place flour, sugar, cornstarch, salt and lemon zest into the bowl of a food processor fitted with a stainless steel blade. Pulse several times to combine ingredients then gradually drop in butter pieces one at a time. Dough will reach a slightly crumbly consistency.

Transfer mixture to buttered 13x9x2-inch (33x23x5cm) baking dish. With fingers, press mixture into the bottom of the dish to form an even layer of crust.

For filling, place all ingredients into a stainless steel bowl and mix lightly.

For crumbles, combine all ingredients and hand mix until crumbles form.

Pour fruit mixture into pan and top with crumbles. Bake for 30 minutes. Let cool at room temperature.

Prepare crème anglaise by creaming egg yolks with sugar. Bring milk and orange zest to a boil, and slowly stir into egg mixture. Gently simmer for about 10 minutes or until cream coats the back of a wooden spoon. Do not allow sauce to boil. Remove from heat, pour into a bowl and stir to cool.

For roasted peaches, in a small sauté pan over medium heat, melt butter and sugar; add peaches and sauté for 2 minutes. Transfer into a greased cookie sheet and bake for 7 minutes or until peaches are tender to the touch. Let cool at room temperature.

Cut cake into individual portions. Place on chilled plates, spoon crème anglaise around and sprinkle with cinnamon powder.

Serve cake with a side dish of vanilla ice cream finished with toasted almonds and a roasted peach.

Serves 10.

CULINARY NOTES:

If the crème anglaise has overcooked and the texture is curdled, try whisking the sauce using a wire whisk first. If this doesn't work, transfer sauce into a bottle and shake well. The action will homogenize the sauce and may produce a smoother texture.

FILLING

1 cup (250 ml) sweetened condensed milk
5 egg yolks
1/2 cup (120 ml) freshly squeezed lime juice

1 (9-inch or 23 cm) pie shell or graham cracker
shell, pre-baked

GARNISH

1/4 cup (60 ml) cream, whipped
Lime zest
10 freshly cut lime slices

KEY LIME PIE

Preheat oven to 350°F or 180°C.

Place condensed milk in a mixing bowl, and beat at low speed, adding egg yolks one at a time.

Add lime juice, and mix thoroughly. Place mixture in a pre-baked pie shell. Bake for 15 minutes or until a skewer inserted comes out clean.

Let cool and refrigerate for 2 hours. Top with whipped cream and sprinkle with lime zest.

Serve on chilled plates. Garnish with lime slices.

Serves 10.

CULINARY NOTES:

It's a well known fact that the Key lime is indigenous to Florida and the "key" ingredient for the state's popular Key lime pie. Forced to substitute condensed milk for fresh – which was scarce before the arrival of the railroad in Florida in 1912 – cooks discovered that the chemical intervention between the condensed milk and the Key lime actually "cooked" the pie without having to bake it.

SOUFFLÉ
1 1/4 cups (300 ml) milk
1/2 cup (120 g) sugar
5 tablespoons (100 g) unsalted butter
1/2 cup (120 g) all-purpose flour, sifted
6 egg yolks
Zest of half an orange
2 tablespoons (30 ml) Grand Marnier®

8 egg whites
1 pinch salt
1/4 cup (60 g) sugar

CRÈME ANGLAISE
6 egg yolks
1/2 cup (120 g) sugar
2 1/2 cups (600 ml) milk
1 vanilla bean, split lengthwise or
1 teaspoon (5 ml) vanilla extract

GARNISH
1/4 cup (60 g) powdered sugar

GRAND MARNIER SOUFFLÉ

Preheat oven to 375°F or 190°C.

Butter soufflé dishes or ramekins and dust with a little sugar. Tilt and tap out excess.

In a medium saucepan, combine milk and sugar and bring to a boil.

In a small saucepan, over medium heat, melt butter and slowly mix in flour. Then stir in milk mixture. Slowly cook over low temperature, until mixture pulls from the saucepan, about 10 minutes. Do not boil. Remove from heat and slowly add egg yolks, one at a time, then orange zest and Grand Marnier. This cream can be made in advance and refrigerated.

In a mixing bowl, beat egg whites and pinch of salt with an electric mixer on medium speed until eggs are frothy. Increase speed to high and gradually add sugar, beating egg whites until they form soft peaks.

Spoon one-third of egg whites into the Grand Marnier mixture and gently mix until the batter is lightened. Fold in remaining egg whites, taking care not to deflate them. Divide the mixture into the soufflé dishes.

Bake for about 20 minutes or until the soufflés have doubled in size and are nicely browned.

Prepare crème anglaise by creaming egg yolks with sugar. Bring milk and pre-cut vanilla bean to a boil, then slowly stir into egg mixture. Gently simmer for about 10 minutes or until cream coats the back of a wooden spoon. Do not allow sauce to boil. Take out vanilla bean. Remove from heat, pour into a bowl, and stir for a minute or two to cool.

Dust the soufflés with powdered sugar and serve immediately with crème anglaise.

Serves 4.

CULINARY NOTES:

We have all seen the soufflé used as a comedy device in television sitcoms. Scenes of frustrated housewives removing a lovely, golden-brown masterpiece from the oven, only to have it collapse before her tear-filled eyes, have been around since the dawn of television.

The soufflé is not as challenging as many people think. It does take practice and you will need to work out the baking time based on your oven's temperature.

To perfect the technique, make a batch of a basic soufflé mix and bake a few "practice soufflés." You will be able to see how the egg mixture rises and to spot where your oven is either too hot or too cool. One step you do not want to overlook is dusting the inside of the soufflé dishes with sugar. The sugar will give the egg mixture something to grab on to as it rises up the side of the dish.

Ingredients

RASPBERRY MOUSSE

2 tablespoons (30 g) sugar
5 egg whites
Pinch salt
1/2 tablespoon (10 g) gelatin powder
1 tablespoon (15 ml) warm water
1/3 cup (90 ml) red berry fruit purée or raspberry
Melba sauce, purchased
1 cup (250 ml) heavy cream, whipped

PASSION FRUIT MOUSSE

2 tablespoons (30 g) sugar
5 egg whites
Pinch salt

1/2 tablespoon (10 g) gelatin powder
1 tablespoon (15 ml) warm water
1/3 cup (90 ml) passion fruit purée or
1/2 cup (120 ml) unsweetened passion fruit
juice reduced by half
1 cup (250 ml) heavy cream, whipped

RASPBERRY COULIS

1 cup (250 g) raspberries
1/4 cup (60 g) sugar
1/4 cup (60 ml) water

MANGO COULIS

1 cup (250 g) diced mango
1/4 cup (60 g) sugar
1/4 cup (60 ml) water

CAKE

1 vanilla sponge cake mix, purchased
and baked as per recipe

GLAZE

1/4 cup (60 ml) mirror glaze, purchased

GARNISH

10 chocolate crescents, purchased
10 chocolate cigarettes, purchased

PASSIONBERRY DUO

For berry mousse, in a small saucepan over low heat, cook sugar until it reaches 250°F or 120°C. Do not boil. In a mixing bowl, beat egg whites and a pinch of salt with an electric mixer on medium speed until eggs are frothy.

Increase speed to high and gradually add cooked sugar, beating egg whites until they form hard peaks.

Dissolve gelatin in water and mix with raspberry purée. Gently fold fruit purée with egg white mixture, then whipped cream. Keep refrigerated while making the passion fruit mousse.

For passion fruit mousse, in a small saucepan over low heat, cook sugar until it reaches 250°F or 120°C. Do not boil. In a mixing bowl, beat egg whites and a pinch of salt with an electric mixer on medium speed until eggs are frothy.

Increase speed to high and gradually add cooked sugar, beating egg whites until they form hard peaks.

Dissolve gelatin in water and mix with passion fruit purée. Gently fold fruit purée with egg white mixture, then whipped cream. Refrigerate for 15 minutes before using.

For raspberry coulis, over medium heat, mix all ingredients in a small saucepan and simmer for 15 minutes. Transfer into a blender and blend until smooth. Strain and refrigerate.

For mango coulis, over medium heat, mix all ingredients in a small saucepan and simmer for 15 minutes. Transfer into a blender and blend until smooth. Strain and refrigerate.

Cut sponge cake into 1/4-inch (1/2 cm) layers. Using a cookie cutter, cut out 8 rounds of cake and place into the base of each mold or ramekins.

Pour berry mousse over cake, half way to the top and refrigerate for at least 1 hour. Once set, top with passion fruit mousse and refrigerate for another hour.

Glaze with mirror glaze and refrigerate for 1/2 hour.

Dip molds into hot water for a few seconds to easily remove cakes from molds.

Drizzle both coulis on chilled plates, arrange cake in the center and garnish with chocolate accents.

Serves 8.

CULINARY NOTES:

What is a passion fruit anyway? Passion fruit is native to Brazil and is so named because the early Spanish Missionaries thought the flower's complex structure and pattern reminded them of symbols associated with the passion of Christ. It was said that the flower contained the lashes received by Christ, the crown of thorns, the column, the five wounds and the three nails.

The fruit is about the size of an egg with red, yellow or purple-brown skin. It has an intense, tart flavor and is used as an additive in juices to enhance the aroma. Both fruit and juice can be found fresh in most supermarkets or ethnic food markets. It is also available canned or frozen.

CHICKEN STOCK

*5 pounds (2.25 kg) chicken bones, including feet and
neck, or 2 roasted chicken carcasses*
3 quarts (2.8 L) cold water
2 carrots, peeled and coarsely sliced
2 medium onions, coarsely chopped
2 stalks celery, coarsely chopped
1 leek, washed and cut into 1/2-inch (1.2 cm) chunks
2 cloves garlic, crushed
2 bay leaves
3 parsley sprigs
1/4 teaspoon (1.5 g) black peppercorns

Place chicken bones into a large pot and pour in cold
water to cover by 2-inches (5 cm). Bring to a boil,
regularly skimming off fat and froth that rise to the
surface.

Once water is boiling, add remaining ingredients,
reduce heat to low, cover and simmer for 2 1/2 to
3 hours, skimming occasionally.

Strain stock through a fine sieve lined with several
layers of cheesecloth and refrigerate, uncovered,
overnight.

Discard congealed layer of fat on the surface and
strain once again into small containers or ice
cube trays.

Use stock immediately or freeze it and use as needed.

Makes 2 1/2 quarts (2.4 L).

FISH STOCK

BOUQUET GARNI
3 sprigs parsley
3 celery leaves
1 sprig thyme
1/4 teaspoon (1.5 g) black peppercorns
1 bay leaf

STOCK
2 tablespoons (30 ml) extra virgin olive oil
*1 pound (450 g) fish bones and heads from any
saltwater fish, except salmon*
1 carrot, peeled and coarsely sliced
1 shallot, coarsely chopped
1 small onion, coarsely chopped
1 stalk celery, coarsely chopped
1 leek, washed and cut into 1/2-inch (1.2 cm) chunks
1 clove garlic, crushed
1/4 cup (60 ml) dry white wine
5 cups (1.2 L) cold water

Prepare bouquet garni by wrapping parsley, celery,
thyme, peppercorn, and bay leaf inside a piece of
cheesecloth and tying it with kitchen string.

In a saucepan over medium heat, warm oil and sauté
fish bones and vegetables for 8 minutes. Add wine
and stir, scraping the bottom of the pan. Add
bouquet garni and enough water to completely cover
fish. Bring to a boil, regularly skimming off fat and
froth that rise to the surface. Reduce heat to low and
simmer for 30 minutes.

Strain stock through a fine sieve lined with several
layers of cheesecloth.

Use stock immediately or freeze it in small containers
and use as needed.

Makes 1 quart (950 ml).

VEGETABLE STOCK

2 tablespoons (30 ml) extra virgin olive oil
1 medium onion, coarsely chopped
1 leek, washed and cut into 1/2-inch (1.2 cm) chunks
1 stalk celery, coarsely chopped
1 turnip, peeled and coarsely chopped
2 carrots, peeled and coarsely chopped
2 tomatoes, peeled, seeded and chopped
1 clove garlic, crushed
3 sprigs parsley
1 sprig thyme
1 bay leaf
1/4 teaspoon (1.5 g) black peppercorns
5 cups (1.2 L) cold water

Heat oil in a stockpot over medium heat. Add
vegetables and sauté for 10 minutes. Do not brown.

Add enough water to completely cover the vegetables.
Reduce heat to low and simmer for 30 minutes.

Strain stock through a fine sieve lined with several
layers of cheesecloth.

Use immediately or freeze it into small containers
and use as needed.

Makes 1 quart (950 ml).

BEEF STOCK

4 pounds (1.8 kg) beef bones
1/2 pound (250 g) veal trimmings
1 onion, coarsely chopped
2 carrots, peeled and coarsely chopped
2 stalks celery, coarsely chopped
1 leek, washed and cut into 1/2-inch (1.2 cm) chunks
1 tablespoon (15 g) tomato paste
2 bay leaves
3 parsley sprigs
1/4 teaspoon (1.5 g) black peppercorns
21/2 quarts (2.4 L) cold water

Preheat oven to 400°F or 200°C.

Place beef bones, veal trimmings, and onion in a roasting pan and roast uncovered for 1 hour or until bones are golden brown.

Transfer to a stockpot. Add remaining ingredients and pour in enough water to cover completely. Bring to a boil, uncovered, over medium heat. Reduce heat to low, and simmer for 8 to 10 hours. Set aside and let cool.

Strain through a fine sieve lined with several layers of cheesecloth.

Use immediately or freeze it in small containers and use as needed.

Makes 2 quarts (1.8 L).

BROWN SAUCE

BOUQUET GARNI
3 sprigs parsley
3 celery leaves
1 sprig thyme
1/4 teaspoon (1.5 g) black peppercorns
1 bay leaf

SAUCE
4 tablespoons (60 g) unsalted butter
2 medium onions, diced
3 carrots, peeled and diced
3 stalks celery, diced
1/3 cup (90 g) all-purpose flour
3 tablespoons (45 g) tomato paste
4 cups (950 ml) beef stock
Salt and freshly ground black pepper

Prepare bouquet garni by wrapping parsley, celery, thyme, peppercorn, and bay leaf inside a piece of cheesecloth and tying it with kitchen string.

In a medium saucepan over high heat, melt butter. Add onion, carrot and celery and sauté for 15 minutes until vegetables are turning golden brown.

Reduce heat to low and add flour, stirring continuously until flour turns brown. Add tomato paste and cook for another 2 minutes.

Gradually whisk in stock, add the bouquet garni and adjust seasoning with salt and pepper. Bring to a boil, regularly skimming off froth that rises to the surface. Simmer for about 45 minutes, until the sauce has reduced by half.

Strain through a fine sieve lined with several layers of cheesecloth.

Use immediately or freeze it in small containers and use as needed.

Makes 2 cups (500 ml).

DEMI-GLACE

1 cup (250 ml) brown sauce
1 cup (250 ml) beef stock
Salt and freshly ground black pepper

In a medium saucepan over medium heat, combine the stocks and simmer for about 30 minutes, until reduced by half.

Strain through a fine sieve lined with several layers of cheesecloth. Adjust seasoning with salt and pepper.

Use demi-glace immediately or freeze it in small containers and use as needed.

Makes 1 cup (250 ml).

Our day done, we gained a whole new appreciation for the word "pleasure."

BEVERAGES

The story of the Mojito cocktail dates back to the sixteenth century when an infamous pirate, Captain Francis Drake, set his eye upon the wealthy city of Havana. He did not take any treasures but instead left something priceless, the Draque, a forerunner of the Mojito cocktail.

Originally, the cocktail was made by combining aguardiente, sugar, lime, and mint. It was not until the mid-nineteenth century, around the same time Don Facindo Bacardi Masso established the original BACARDI® Rum company, that rum replaced aguardiente and the Draque evolved into the Mojito cocktail.

To this day, a true Mojito cocktail can only be made with BACARDI® Rum.

BACARDI® MOJITO
The hint of mint, a mix of sugar and lime, BACARDI® Mojito cocktails finish fresh and clean.

MOJITO

2 oz. (6 cl) BACARDI® Superior rum

3 mint leaves

4 lime wedges

1 oz. (3 cl) Monin Mojito mint mix

1 oz. (3 cl) club soda

Muddle mint leaves and lime in a tall glass. Cover with Monin Mojito mint mix and fill glass with ice. Add BACARDI® Superior rum and stir.

Top off with club soda and garnish with fresh mint sprigs.

BACARDI®

DESERT PEAR MARGARITA

1¹/₄ oz. (3.75 cl) Patrón Tequila

1 oz. (3 cl) Monin Desert Pear syrup

¹/₂ oz. (1.5 cl) triple sec

2 oz. (6 cl) Island Oasis® Margarita Mix

Fill shaker with ice and add all ingredients. Shake and pour in glass. Garnish.

CAIPIRINHA

1¹/₄ oz. (3.75 cl) Cacacha

1 oz. (25 g) sugar

5 lime wedges

Muddle all ingredients, pour into cocktail shaker filled with ice, shake over ice and pour into highball glass. Garnish with lime wedges.

CARIBBEAN COOLER

1 1/2 oz. (4.5 cl) BACARDI® Coco Rum

1/2 oz. (1.5 cl) Triple Sec

1 1/2 oz. (4.5 cl) orange juice

1/2 oz. (1.5 cl) Rose's® Lime Juice

1 oz. (3 cl) Sprite®

Fill cocktail shaker with ice. Pour all ingredients into the shaker except for the Sprite®. Spindle mix and pour into a poco grande glass.

Top off with Sprite® and garnish with an orange peel.

GOLDEN MARGARITA

1 1/4 oz. (3.75 cl) Cuervo®
Gold Tequila

/4 oz. (2.25 cl) Cointreau®

3 oz. (9 cl) Island Oasis®
Margarita mix

Combine all ingredients in a cocktail shaker with ice. Spindle mix and pour into a salt-rimmed poco margarita glass. Garnish with orange wedge and lime wedge.

LOVE CONNECTION

1 1/2 oz. (4.5 cl) BACARDI® Gold Rum

1 1/2 oz. (4.5 cl) Island Oasis® Pina Colada mix

1 1/2 oz. (4.5 cl) Island Oasis® Strawberry mix

1 1/2 oz. (4.5 cl) Island Oasis® Mango mix

Blend 1/2 oz. (1.5 cl) rum with each of the mixes and ice. Layer each blend into a hurricane glass in the following order: Strawberry, Pina Colada, Mango.

Serve with a colorful straw.

WILDBERRY LAVA COLADA

1 1/4 oz. (3.75 cl) BACARDI® Razz

3 oz. (9 cl) Island Oasis® Pina Colada mix

1 oz. (3 cl) Island Oasis® Wildberry mix

Blend BACARDI® Razz and Pina Colada mix with ice until smooth.

Pour Island Oasis® Wildberry into a glass and pour the blended mixture on top. Garnish with pineapple leaves and blackberries.

BBC

1 1/4 oz. (3.75 cl) Baileys® Irish Cream

2 oz. (6 cl) Island Oasis® Banana mix

2 oz. (6 cl) Island Oasis® Pina Colada mix

Blend all ingredients with ice into a smooth consistency. Rim the inside of a poco grande glass with chocolate sauce and pour the blended mix into the glass. Garnish with chocolate.

ISLAND OASIS
The World's Finest Frozen Drink™

ROYAL BEER

A Royal Caribbean private label beer, this blonde Belgian Ale is smooth and refreshing with hints of lemon. A true treasure!

While exploring the depths of the Caribbean Sea, adventurers discovered amongst a sunken galleon's treasures a Legendary Belgian Ale recipe. Brought back to a renowned Belgian brewery, this time-honored recipe is now being brewed exclusively for Royal Caribbean International.

SAPPHIRE-TINI

1/2 oz. (1.5 cl) Blue Curacao

3/4 oz. (2.25 cl) BACARDI®
Coco Rum

3/4 oz. (2.25 cl) banana liqueur

2 oz. (6 cl) pineapple juice

Fill a cocktail shaker with ice.
Pour all ingredients into
cocktail shaker. Shake and
strain into a chilled blue
Gemtini glass.

AMBER-TINI

1/2 oz. (1.5 cl) Grenadine

1/2 oz. (1.5 cl) cranberry juice

Shake over ice and strain into a chilled
amber Gemtini glass.

1 1/4 oz. (3.75 cl) Peach Schnapps

3/4 oz. (2.25 cl) Grey Goose®
La Vanille Vodka

1 oz. (3 cl) orange juice

Shake over ice and strain and pour on top
of the Grenadine mixture.

Gem-tini Collection

EMERALD-TINI

3/4 oz. (2.25 cl) Grey Goose® Vodka

1 1/4 oz. (3.75 cl) Sour Apple Schnapps

2 oz. (6 cl) sweet & sour

1/2 oz. (1.5 cl) Monin Granny Smith syrup

Fill a cocktail shaker with ice. Pour all ingredients into cocktail shaker. Shake and strain into a chilled green Gemtini glass.

RUBY-TINI

1 1/4 oz. (3.75 cl) BACARDI® Limon

1 oz. (3 cl) cranberry juice

1 oz. (3 cl) grapefruit juice

1/4 oz. (0.75 cl) Simple Syrup

Fill a cocktail shaker with ice. Pour all ingredients into cocktail shaker. Shake and strain into a chilled red Gemtini glass. Garnish with sugar-dusted berries.

MUDSLIDE

¹/4 oz. (0.75 cl) Kahlúa®

¹/2 oz. (1.5 cl) Bailey's®
Irish Cream

¹/4 oz. (0.75 cl) Grey
Goose® Vodka

1 oz. (3 cl) milk

In a shot glass, pour each ingredient in order listed. Use the back of a spoon to carefully layer each ingredient on top of the other.

BANANA BOAT

¹/4 oz. (0.75 cl) Kahlúa®

¹/4 oz. (0.75 cl) banana liqueur

¹/4 oz. (0.75 cl) Tia Maria®

¹/4 oz. (0.75 cl) BACARDI® Select

In a shot glass, pour each ingredient in order listed. Use the back of a spoon to carefully layer each ingredient on top of the other.

CAPPUCCINO

1 shot espresso

Steamed milk

Foam

Pour a shot of espresso in a large coffee cup. Pour hot steamed milk on top of the espresso, filling the cup about 2/3. Add foam of the milk on top and top off with a sprinkle of cinnamon.

CAPTAIN'S CALL

1 oz. (3 cl) Kahlúa®

1/4 oz. (0.75 cl) Cognac

Freshly brewed coffee

Whipped cream

Chocolate shavings

Using a glass Irish coffee mug, pour the Kahlúa and Cognac in the glass. Top off with hot coffee and mound with whipped cream. Sprinkle chocolate shavings on top.

ROYAL DELIGHT

1/2 oz. (1.5 cl) Grand Marnier®

1/2 oz. (1.5 cl) Bailey's® Irish Cream

1/2 oz. (1.5 cl) Tuaca® Liqueur

1 shot espresso

Pour all ingredients over ice into a cocktail shaker. Shake and strain into a chilled martini glass.

COOKING TERMS

AL DENTE: Italian for "to the tooth" and is used to describe a food that is cooked until it gives a slight resistance when one bites into it.

BLANCHING: Cooking a food very briefly and partially in boiling water or hot fat as part of a combination cooking method. Usually used to loosen peels from vegetables and fruits.

BLENDING: A mixing method in which two or more ingredients are combined until they are evenly distributed; a spoon, rubber spatula, whisk or electric mixer with its paddle attachment can be used.

BOIL: To cook in water or other liquid at an approximate temperature of 212°F or 100°C at sea level.

BOUQUET GARNI: A blend of herbs and vegetables tied in a bundle with twine and used to flavor stocks, soups, sauces and stews.

BROIL: To cook by heat radiating from an overhead source.

CARAMELIZE: Fruits and vegetables with natural sugars can be caramelized by sautéing, roasting or grilling, giving them a sweet flavor and golden glaze.

CHIFFONADE: To slice into thin strips or shreds.

CLARIFIED BUTTER: Purified butterfat; the butter is melted and water and milk solids are removed: also known as drawn butter.

CONCASSÉ: To chop coarsely.

DEGLAZE: To swirl or stir a liquid like wine or stock in a pan to dissolve cooked food particles remaining on the bottom, using the mixture as the base for the sauce.

DEGREASE: To skim the fat from the top of a liquid.

DICE: To cut food into cubes.

DREDGE: To coat food with flour, breadcrumbs or cornmeal before frying.

FLAMBÉ: Pour warmed spirits such as brandy, whisky or rum over foods such as fruits or meat and then ignite it.

FOLD: To combine a light ingredient like egg whites with a much heavier mixture like whipped cream.

FRY: To cook in hot fat.

GELATIN: A colorless, odorless and flavorless mixture of proteins made from animal bones, connective tissues and certain algae; when dissolved in warm liquid it forms a jelly-like substance used as a thickener for desserts, cold soups and certain sauces.

GRILL: Cooking in which the heat source is located beneath the rack on which the food is placed.

JULIENNE: Foods cut into matchstick shapes.

MACERATE: Soaking fruits in liquid, such as brandy or other alcoholic ingredients, so they absorb that flavor. Macerate can also be fruits sprinkled with sugar, which draws out the natural juices of the fruit, creating a syrup.

MARINADE: A seasoned liquid in which raw foods are soaked or coated to absorb flavors and/or become tender before cooking.

MINCE: To cut or chop a food finely.

MONTER: To finish a sauce by swirling or whisking butter until it is melted.

PAN-BROIL: To cook food uncovered and without

PAN-FRY: To cook food in a moderate amount of h fat, uncovered.

POACH: To gently cook food submerged in a simmering liquid.

PURÉE: To process food to achieve a smooth pulp.

REDUCE: To cook by simmering a liquid until the quantity decreases by evaporation.

REFRESH: The process of submerging food (usuall vegetables) in cold water to cool it quickly and prev further cooking.

SEAR: To brown a food quickly over high heat.

SEASON: Adding flavor to foods. Season can also m to coat the surface of a new pot or pan with vegetal oil and placing in a hot oven for about 1 hour. As th oil burns off, the carbon residue fills in the small p and groves of the pan's surface making a smooth fin that helps prevent food from sticking.

SIMMER: To maintain the temperature of a liquid j below the boiling point.

STIR-FRY: To cook food over high heat with little fa while stirring constantly and briskly.

INDEX

Left to right: Josef Jungwirth, *Director, Culinary Operations*; Ken Taylor, *Director, Restaurant Operations*; Frank Weber, *Vice President, Food & Beverage Operations*; Corinne Lewis, *Manager, Catering & Retail Operations*; Bob Midyette, *Director, Beverage Operations*.

This cookbook is dedicated to the esteemed culinary professionals responsible for creating the vast array of gourmet meals served in our main dining rooms, specialty and buffet restaurants on board.

The discovery of a new dish does more for the happiness of mankind than the discovery of a new star.
Brillat – Savarin, 1838

Very Special Thanks To…
Our Chairman and CEO, Richard Fain; President, Adam Goldstein; and Sr. VP Hotel Operations, Lisa Bauer for their continued support of *Savor*.

Additional recognition to Henry Lopez, Director Corporate Purchasing and his team and Jessica Correa, AVP, Market Planning & Product Development. Without their involvement, this book would never have come to fruition.

Our Senior Chefs and Executive Chefs, for their dedication to culinary excellence. The Hotel Directors, F&B Managers, Maitre D's, Bar Managers and the entire Food & Beverage and Service teams on board, who make it all happen…24/7/365.

Manager, Catering & Retail Operations, Corinne Lewis, who organized, developed and coordinated the project; our Director of Culinary Operations, Josef Jungwirth, for his creative contributions and our Director of Beverage Operations, Bob Midyette, for his delectable libations.

Our Food, Beverage and Service teams shoreside, Cary Butcher, Clay Carrier, Lisa Delgado, Jessica Fleisher, Giovanni Guido, Fritz Halbedl, Kelle Jones, Michele Nyakas, Kendra Prince, Beth Sadowsky, Ken Taylor and Carmen Vergara.

Our sponsors, Island Oasis, Seattle's Best Coffee and Bacardi; the following business partners: Albert Uster Import, Chocolate á la Carte, the dedicated Tad Ware & Company Publishing and Photography team for their creativity and support, and photographer Greg Schneider for the galley and restaurant shots.